1-5-76

PSYCHIC CITY: CHICAGO

BY BRAD STEIGER

Psychic City: Chicago
Other Worlds, Other Universes (WITH JOHN WHITE)
Medicine Talk
Medicine Power
Atlantis Rising
Revelation: The Divine Fire
Irene Hughes on Psychic Safari
The Psychic Feats of Olof Jonsson
Mysteries of Time and Space
Secrets of Kahuna Magic
Minds Through Space and Time
Know the Future Today
Other Lives
The Mind Travellers
In My Soul I Am Free
UFO Breakthrough
The Enigma of Reincarnation
ESP: Your Sixth Sense
The Unknown
Strange Guests

Psychic City: Chicago

Doorway to Another Dimension

Brad Steiger

DOUBLEDAY & COMPANY, INC.
GARDEN CITY, NEW YORK
1976

Library of Congress Cataloging in Publication Data

Steiger, Brad.
   Psychic City: doorway to another dimension.

   1. Psychical research—Chicago. 2. Occult
sciences—Chicago. 3. Psychical research—
Biography. 4. Occult sciences—Biography.
I. Title.
BF1028.5.U6S74   133'.09773'11
ISBN 0-385-01362-0

The selections in Chapter Two, from Curtis Fuller's column "I See by the Papers," FATE magazine, August 1967, and in Chapter Twelve, from Tom C. Lyle's review of Frank Rudolph Young's CYCLOMANCY: THE SECRET OF PSYCHIC POWER CONTROL are quoted by special permission from FATE magazine.

Designed by LAURENCE ALEXANDER

Library of Congress Catalog Card Number 74–33663
Copyright © 1976 by Other Dimensions, Inc.

CONTENTS

— I

North America's Most Psychic City

BACK IN THE EARLY 1960s when I was aggressively studying spontaneous phenomena, mediumship, and the field of psychic inquiry in general, I began to notice a curious pattern. Regardless of where I may have set out on my psychic safaris, I always ended up in Chicago.

I soon learned that an overwhelming number of major psychics live in Chicago, that nearly all the principal spiritual and psychic organizations maintain their head offices in Chicago, and that the greatest series of important psychic events and happenings were scheduled for Chicago. There came to be no question in my mind that the "toddling" town was also a remarkably "tuned-in" town. Although there are fine psychic-sensitives and men and women attuned to the spiritual vibration in every metropolis and village on the continent, I came to

North America's Most Psychic City

realize early in my investigative career that Chicago is truly North America's most psychic city.

As an upper-Midwesterner, I suppose that I have always regarded Chicago as my capital city. Saint Louis helped win the West; Minneapolis and Saint Paul are the friendly twins up North; everything is up to date in Kansas City; but Chicago is my Big City.

Even as a boy on our Iowa farm I was touched by the mystique of Chicago. As I watched the livestock being loaded into huge semitrailer trucks, I knew that their final destination, their Valhalla, their happy grazing ground, would be Chicago.

Aunt Clarice, who had toured with an opera company, lived in Chicago; and she had married an honest-to-God boxer whom my husky father could punch in the stomach without knocking his "wind" out. Aunt Delia lived there too, and three girl cousins; and when they visited their relatives' Iowa farms, it was as if they had come from some faraway and fabled emerald city.

Chicago was Hog Butcher, Hoodlum, Houri, Haberdasher, Hot-Jazz Musician, Hosteler, and Hub for the railroads; but since it sprawled in Illinois, and not New York, we all knew that it was really just an overgrown Midwestern town that was locked into an eternity of Saturday nights.

My wife, kids, and I even took a brief sabbatical from our Iowa village and hilly fields in 1969 and attempted an exploratory immigration to Psychic Chicago. Although we thoroughly enjoyed the opportunity to tune our receptors into the city's vibrations to an even greater degree than before, it took us only six months to verify that my Medicine Power and my art function best in a pastoral environment. The psychic emanations from those concrete canyons were inspiring, and the power place that is Chicago can surely serve as a psychic oasis to any sojourner seeking metaphysical truths; but for what it is that makes my visions come into clearer focus, I need always to embrace the Earth Mother in those places where she does not wear garments of steel and asphalt.

Why has Chicago become North America's first city in terms of the assemblage of high-quality psychics and the number of spiritually oriented organizations of national and international reputation that have collected there?

Have the reasons to do solely with geographical location and a peculiar combination of ethnic amalgamations?

Or is Chicago a psychic power place, crossed by spiritual ley lines, which has received special grooming by preternatural forces for a unique role in the emerging New Age?

"I feel Chicago is the only city that has a balanced energy," Matin Ciani of Para-Dimensions, Inc., told me. "I feel that the energy emanating from Chicago is a correlated energy. Chicago has a nucleus, a core. Its energy is not scattered the way it is in Los Angeles or New York.

"For another thing, the professional jealousies among psychics aren't as strong here as they are in some cities. Chicago is a hub of controlled psychical manifestations."

Vanessa Whitlock of Thee Satanic Church feels that the concentration of so many high-quality professional psychics in one area certainly bears a message for everyone: "We have Joe DeLouise, Irene Hughes, Henry Rucker—these people are phenomenal. There was that fantastic gentleman who just died, Rev. Clifford Royse. And there are so many others! When they all gather in one location, that's got to be telling you something!

"Chicago is where the core or the hub of the New Age is beginning, and it will branch out from here. If you want to talk about strides forward in parapsychology, if you want to discuss prophecy, if you want to talk about removing fear from the masses, these things are going to be happening here. Chicago is where individuals are going to find the truth.

"In Chicago, those of us in spiritual work are all laboring for the same goal: lifting man's level of awareness. Whatever we can contribute as a whole or on an individual basis, we do so. We help one another to aid everyone in getting together to bring all of Mankind forward. None of us can do this on an individual basis. There is no single path; there is no one right way.

"Yes, I have the Satanic Church, but I exchange ideas and philosophies with everyone in all other groups. We host rap sessions here, where people can come in right off the street to seek knowledge. We tell everyone who stops in, whether out of serious motivation or idle curiosity, that we are not asking anyone to change his religion. We are only asking people to look inward and to realize that they are not utilizing all of their mental faculties. Take what we have to offer, we tell them; absorb it like a sponge; then let us send you elsewhere."

Dr. Joseph Pinkston feels that he was led to Chicago by divine guidance.

"I have had success in Chicago with everything that I have undertaken in the psychic field," he said. "People here just seem to accept the spiritual powers more than they do in other parts of the country. We have a lot of outstanding radio and television people who give us a fair hearing, and medical departments and other university personnel seem to be open toward the field. This kind of atmosphere inspires outstanding spiritual leadership and spiritual phenomena."

Dr. Pinkston also took note of the spirit of unity and cooperation that exists among psychic-sensitives in Chicago: "The vibrations here are much stronger than in other parts of the country. And there is little jealousy among the psychics here. We can all get together and discuss the things that happen to us. It is good to get the different views of other psychics. We are working toward coming together as one and accomplishing great things in the psychic field."

Ruth Brooks, Programs Unlimited, plans psychically oriented meetings for a great number of people and brings in speakers from all parts of the country. When she moved to Chicago from Detroit, in 1966, she became deeply involved with Spiritual Frontiers Fellowship and became acquainted with numerous parapsychologists and psychics, as well as clergymen, who were interested in interpreting the current public interest in psychism for the churches—especially where it relates to prayer, healing, personal survival, and meditation. Because of her public-relations background, Ruth found several well-known psychics asking her to arrange lectures, tours, and media appearances for them. Although she had never before directed a lecture bureau, such a move seemed right.

"Los Angeles might be close in interest," Mrs. Brooks commented, "but things seem to be happening most in the Chicago area. Such fine groups as Spiritual Frontiers Fellowship are located here, and we have some outstanding psychics who have come to the foreground of public attention.

"At the same time, Chicago has a number of strong, powerful churches, which are not necessarily liberally oriented, but which, I am certain, contribute to the strong aura of spirituality which Chicago emanates. Chicago seems to be filled with people who want to grow; and I feel these people will expand and grow so rapidly that they will hardly know what has happened to them. This is good. I think that all of us must become more spiritually oriented and emanate love or we will be destroyed.

"We are all neighbors on this planet, and we must learn to live in peace. In order to have peace, we must have love, believe in God and in his guidance, and become more spiritually oriented in our approach to life."

Frederic De Arechaga, of the Sabaean Religious Order of Amn, offered these interesting observations of factors that he feels may contribute to the spiritual power of Psychic Chicago:

"I personally feel more comfortable in Chicago than anywhere else because the North Magnetic Pole passes right through the city. This, by the way, is a peculiarity of zero degrees, which also passes through Cairo.

"According to ancient texts, what makes a city sacred is not so much its religious influences as a peculiar magnetism which seems to be centered in the place.

"From the symbological, archetypal point of view, Chicago is visited by all four winds and all four seasons. I did not think there was any place like this in the world. These peculiar things of nature and topography have a great deal to do with the magnetic influence that is here.

"Although Chicago is a city of churches and a center for many orthodox church bodies, even the conventional members of organized congregations seem to be tolerant and concerned with learning. There are not the neuroses of New York, the lethargies of Florida, and the theatrics of California. Chicago seems to be somehow more centered and balanced.

"Perhaps the West Coast is more often identified with

the Occult in the mind of the average man. This is especially true after the Sharon Tate murders. But the greatest amount of serious, nonsensationalistic work is occurring in Chicago.

"Chicago has a very Babylonian appearance. The city is very sprawled out. It is made up of large, square brick buildings. There are terraced gardens. There is a river running through it. Like Babylon, Chicago is a trade center. Babylon had so many bulls and calves that they were impossible to count. Babylon was the city of the bull. Chicago has been the center of the cattle market. Chicago is very much like Babylon restored."

I am certain that by now—and since Frederic De Arechaga has reminded you—many of my readers have begun to question the intensity of Chicago's psychic vibrations over those of Los Angeles—or for that matter, the entire West Coast.

There are, of course, several outstanding psychic-sensitives who make their home in California, but it is my contention that it is the well-publicized activities of organized cults, sects, and proselytzing Eastern religions that make it appear to the average man or woman that the West Coast is the center of metaphysical work in the United States. At the same time, certain fringe groups have emulated the philosophical tenets of serious spiritual pathways, warped them and distorted them to fit their own questionable ideologies, then set about directing a great deal of media attention toward their negative actions and foolishly iconoclastic statements. On too many unfortunate occasions, these same fringe groups have permitted their essentially anti-social, self-serving, love-destructive activities to erupt into senseless and horrible acts of death and violence.

Yes, it is true: *The New Age will belong to everyone.*

Yes, it is true: *The vibrations that elevate consciousness are everywhere.*

Yes, it is true: *There are beautiful workers of spirit residing throughout the United States.*

I quite agree with Eursula Royse of the Foundation for Truth, who told me: "Any place can have a good vibration for you if you are teaching what you believe. Regardless of what city or state or country you live in, there are people who have the same needs, the same wants. We're all human beings, and we radiate the same things. We're going to attract to us that which we are."

But it is my opinion—and this book contains the documentation—that the psychic center of our nation lies in Chicago. Certainly there are many power places—areas of spiritual energy concentration—scattered throughout the North American continent. The Amerindian people know of many. Perhaps you have the requisite sensitivity to have identified such a sacred spot near you. But in this particular segment of time and space, the center of the psychic cyclone is Chicago.

I asked Dr. J. Gordon Melton, historian of religion, Director of the Institute for the Study of American Religions, if he agreed with my premise.

DR. J. GORDON MELTON: There is an oft-repeated myth that California is *the* home for the weirdest religious fringe groups in America. David St. Clair quotes a San Francisco astrologer as saying, "Didn't you hear that God picked up the United States right under the East Coast and lifted it into the air? When he did, the loose nuts rolled down into California."

How California developed such a reputation is shrouded in history. Early observation of the nonconventional religious bodies branded California as a unique home of the weird, the fanatical, and the bizarre. The myth has been bolstered by wide media coverage of a few incidents such as the "kidnaping" of Aimee Semple McPherson, the trial of Frank Ballard (of the I AM Movement), the explosive death of Krishna Venta, the naming of an official witch of Los Angeles County; by 1972 (in *The Psychic World of California*) David St. Clair could honestly say, "California, America's most psychic, occult, and mystic state. California, the strangest state in the nation. Everyone admits it. No one disputes it."

Numerous authors have asked "why," but few if any have inquired into whether the myth was true or not. Certainly there is strong evidence to the contrary, and there are hard questions to be considered before any decision is reached.

The first observation about California is its continuity with the rest of the religious life of the United States. A quick glance at the telephone book of any California community reveals the strong support given by residents to the dominant religious bodies of the nation. As in any eastern city, Roman Catholics, Methodists, Baptists, Presbyterians, and Lutherans are in abundance. The fundamentalist, pentecostal, and pietist sects imported from the East are also present. In the residential areas of California towns, one would catch little hint that anything out of the ordinary was happening religiously.

Secondly, if one visited any large eastern or midwestern city, one would find functioning there a wide range of nonconventional religious groups. In Chicago, for instance, are "congregations" of the Bahais, Zen Buddhists, Moslems (three varieties), The True Temple of Solomon Church, Ideal Love and Faith Temple, the School of Human Dignity, and the Vivikananda Vedanta Society. These are listed in the phone book. Others one could visit include the Hare Krishna Temple, the Divine Light Mission, The Pagan Way, the Sabaean Society, and numerous psychic and spiritualist groups. California is in no way unique in its hosting of nonconformist religious groups, nor does it by any means have an exclusive claim on them. Is there some reason, then, why California has been branded as the "cult capital," and is there any truth in the claim?

The reason can be accounted for in several ways. First, Southern California's religious groups are associated with Hollywood and the movie industry.

Many Californian groups have played to the news-hungry press. Movie stars who associate with a nonconventional religious body are a major news item. Most recently, Mia Farrow's attachment to Transcendental Meditation and Sharon Tate's murder were powerful image makers.

Secondly, the presence of an oriental population concentrated in the West added to the myth.

Southern California had no more diverse groups than other areas, but a number were Asiatic in origin: Buddhist, Shinto, etc. Such groups center on elaborate temples, unfamiliar ideas, and mystical experiences, and lend themselves to media coverage more easily than the eastern European, black, and Puerto Rican groups of New York.

New York City is home to some religious bodies that certainly could compete with California in nonconventionality—Voodoo Santería, Witchcraft, and possibly more bishops representing fewer congregations than anywhere else on earth. Yet not even the presence of the New York *Times* has been able to offset the California media.

Finally, there is an element of a self-fulfilling image involved in the myth.

As numerous writers have repeated the myth, some people promoting it have believed it and have come to California expecting to find or help create the reality behind the image. In the years since World War II, California has become a haven for transients seeking their own particular Kingdom of Heaven. In the 1960s they flocked to Haight-Ashbury and the Sunset Strip only to disperse around the country within a few years. But enough stayed to add to the image.

If, as Dr. Melton suggests, California's reputation as a hotbed of psychic activity is largely due to the ofttimes questionable efforts of the image makers, then the resultant stereotype of California as a kind of national asylum for dissenters—both secular and civil—must surely wear on the residents of that state. Images, of course, can become very powerful (perhaps even archetypal) things unto themselves.

It was a Chicago sensitive, whom for purposes of this book I shall call Wanda, who told me that it had been Chicago's image as the home of gangsters and prohibition violence that had called down special divine interaction to begin transforming it into the psychic center of our nation.

"Everybody in Europe, Asia, and Africa has heard the word 'Chicago,'" Wanda said. "They don't know where New York is or any names associated with it, but they all know names like Capone, Dillinger, Elliot Ness. They know the

North America's Most Psychic City

atomic bomb that fell on Hiroshima was manufactured in Chicago. They've all seen the televised demonstrations at the Democratic Convention. They have heard of Mayor Daley.

"As a youngster I lived for a time in Europe, and I was impressed by the fact that people throughout the world seem to associate Chicago with organized crime, corruption, gangsterism. People will say, 'Oh, you come from Chicago. Bang! Bang! Bang!' And they become disappointed when you defend Chicago and tell them that there is much more to the city than violence.

"All this negativity has been projected on Chicago for so long! And remember, people don't actually have to be here to saturate the area with negativity. They can mentally project it.

"So now begins the Aquarian Age, a new age. Divinity concentrates on the worst of circumstances, not the best. Divinity comes down and assumes responsibilities in the most criminal, the most negative of places. Chicago is the central point where this actualization is occurring today.

"Astrologically, the Aquarian Age has Leo opposite Aquarius. Chicago is a Leo city. Four fixed points are coming to the horizon: Aquarius, Leo, Taurus, and Scorpio. All the countries and cities that are influenced or ruled by those signs are going to assume prominent roles in the New Age.

"But Chicago is the foremost city that is ruled by those signs. All over the world, astrologers and psychics centralize Chicago as a very potent spot in the Aquarian Age.

"And we've got seed people here in Chicago. Seed people in all levels of city government, all levels of education, many aspects of medicine, the conventional clergy, and all kinds of businessmen. We've got some of the great psychic sensitives, yes; but we have an entire city that is becoming turned on to New Age consciousness!"

This book will seek to acquaint the reader with some of those key seed people of the New Age and, at the same time, attempt to analyze the vibratory energy pattern that comprises Psychic Chicago.

—2

Chicago's Fate— Magazine, That Is

ANY ANSWER THAT WOULD seek to explain why Chicago is North America's most psychic city without including reference to *Fate* magazine would be woefully incomplete. Surely this monthly compendium of articles dealing with "the strange and the unknown" has done more to popularize psychical research and the borderline sciences than any other single publication. This compact little journal has been publishing articles on UFOs, ghosts, monsters, ancient astronauts, healing, and Fortean phenomena since 1948. Try to come up with a new, never-before-published idea on the occult, the paranormal, the bizarre, and you can just bet that *Fate* carried numerous articles on your "new slant" back in the 1950s.

It may be disappointing to many of *Fate*'s long-time readers to learn that the magazine is not produced in some decaying Victorian mansion with a décor inspired by an old Universal horror movie. Highland House, at 500 Hyacinth Place, Highland Park, is unabashedly modern and Curtis and Mary Margaret Fuller, publisher and editor, are unapologetically straight mid-Americans.

"Oh, Brad, you've let your hair grow longer and you've grown a mustache since we last saw you," Mary Margaret Fuller greeted me. She is tall, attractive, twinkle-eyed, and she looks just as healthy as the daughter of a former college athletic coach should. "I've been trying to talk Curt into letting his hair grow over the ears, but he claims it tickles him too much."

Within moments we are joined by Curtis Fuller, hair trimmed conventional business-executive style. It would only seem fair if he at least wore an ankh medallion about his neck instead of a conservative tie, but Curt Fuller would feel as awkward wearing such ostentatious "occult" jewelry as he would letting his hair grow over his ears.

I am certain that many Aquarian Age enthusiasts must feel just a trifle betrayed upon meeting Curt and Mary, because they just do not seem "into" the occult-metaphysical scene in any kind of readily identifiable way. However, they maintain that the strange phenomena they report in *Fate* are but a part of the real world; therefore, there is no reason why either the material in their journal or their personal life styles should suggest other than a holistic view of reality.

I began our interview by asking when *Fate* magazine began.

CURT FULLER: The first issue was brought out in the spring of 1948 by Ray Palmer and me. We both came from Ziff-Davis Publishing Company. Ray had been the fiction editor, and I was editor of *Flying* magazine. Ziff-Davis wanted to move to New York. Ray didn't want to go, and neither did I.

We didn't have a lot of money, so we decided that if we started our own magazine, it would have to have newsstand potential. A Chicago publisher, Gilbert Meites, let Ray and me use his offices, and in a sense, acted as a front for us. He acquainted us with printers and distributors and gave us some information about basic methods of publishing. *Fate*'s first print run was about a hundred thousand copies. We sold about 50 per cent of the run—something you can't do today with an established magazine!

Since Ray Palmer had been a well-known science-fiction editor, was there any discussion as to whether Fate *might be a combination fact-fiction magazine?*

CURT: The original concept of the magazine was mostly Ray's. He had come off the Richard Shaver mystery with its deroes and teroes and underworld kingdoms, and he thought there was an opportunity for a magazine based on Fortean phenomena to make it.

MARY FULLER: Then, too, you were hung up on flying saucers. In 1947, when Kenneth Arnold first saw those things, you spent a lot of time, as editor of *Flying* magazine, interviewing pilots and air-force personnel who were saying they were seeing these things.

CURT: I spent a lot of time at Wright Field, where the air-force research arm, which later became NASA, was located. All they could do was refer me to the works of Charles Fort. We didn't understand much about the psychic field in those days.

Mary and I once discussed your early packaging problems with Fate *and the trouble you had over your cover art.* [*"Report from the Readers,"* Fate, *November 1952: "I read frequently on the busses and crowded streetcars, but never again will I read* Fate *in public. One drunk leaned over a couple of passengers and whistled at 'Ishtar—Goddess of Love.' "—Virginia Vasich, Baltimore, Md.*]

CURT: If we did a Cretan story, we did a naked girl over the horns of a bull—which isn't fiction, by any means.

But whether Cretan maid or Ishtar or Polynesian girl dancing in front of a Kahuna, strands of her long, flowing hair were always discreetly placed over her otherwise naked torso.

MARY: If we didn't, they sued us in Canada!

CURT: Once we were actually fined for running a statue of Venus de Milo *inside* the book! But you see, we were really searching in those days for material, and we were struggling to survive on the newsstands.

MARY: There were no other publications in this country —and very few abroad—to offer us any kind of guidance or precedent.

CURT: Nor were we well acquainted with the field. Initially we made an arrangement with the British magazine *Prediction,* and we bought a lot of U.S.-rights material from them.

What is your relationship with British Fate?

MARY: At the present time there is no relationship. They've folded. We are now looking for a new British publisher. We've had letters from several who are interested, so there will be another British *Fate.*

What is the formula that makes Fate *work so well?*

MARY: I just remarked to a very good friend last week that I wished I knew how it worked so well. Every time a new magazine in the field comes out, I say to myself, "How fast can a girl from Johnson Creek [Wisconsin] run?"

CURT: Of course, Brad, you are aware that we do publish magazines in the camping and mobile-home interest areas here at Clark and Woodall.

Yes, I am, but they are magazines which sell themselves to specialized interest groups, and their editorial content would remain constant and conventional. But how do you decide on the proper ingredient mix for such a publication as Fate? *Did* either of you have a predilection toward this field?

MARY: No, not at all. Curt and I are both trained in journalism from the University of Wisconsin. In the early days of *Fate,* I never even came into the office. I worked with my typewriter home on my bed, determined to get over tuberculosis. In the early 1950s, I set out to sell real estate—which I loved. Then, in about 1955, Curt asked me if I would come into the office for a couple of months.

CURT: Ray Palmer and I were alternating those early issues under the pseudonym of Robert M. Webster.

Aha! I was about to ask about Mr. Webster's role in the formative years of Fate!

MARY: Well, after Curt put me in the office with no authority, I found that I was becoming more and more responsible for putting out the entire magazine. That is a very unfortunate position to be in. I wasn't the editor; I had no authority; but I got to do all the work. Then I would read in the newspaper that Robert M. Webster had given a talk on such and such a topic, and I would froth at the mouth in a quiet sort of way. At last I told Curt that I felt it was not to be borne. That is when my name went on the masthead and Robert M. Webster retired to Europe.

CURT: Ray had suffered a terrible accident, which is why I brought Mary into the office in the first place. For a while it was touch and go whether he would live; and if he lived, whether or not he would be paralyzed. Ray made a recovery; he is a very gallant guy.

We bought out Ray's stock in *Fate,* and he moved to Wisconsin, where he bought a farm and a printing plant. In short order he had created *Flying Saucers* and *Search* magazines.

MARY: We have remained friends. He stays with us when he comes to Chicago, which has not been for a long time, and we stop in Amherst to see him. I am a Palmer fan along with the rest of his readers.

What are your plans for Fate *in the immediate future?*

MARY: As I said, I don't really know what I do, but if you should ask me specifically what am I doing with a certain department in the magazine, I know exactly what I am doing with it.

Basically, I am publishing what is believable to me. Not according to what I know to be true, but what is *possibly* believable. I publish what I am interested in.

We run a survey two or three times a year to see what our readers want to see in *Fate.* Witchcraft is one of the things that *Fate* readers really don't care for very much. At the present time, our readers seem most interested in ancient civilizations. Flying saucers run a close second as a topic of interest. They love Curt's column "I See by the Papers." They are fond of "True Mystic Experiences." They like "Report from the Readers." A great many of them like David Techter's book-review column.

We can't always cover a subject in depth, the way we might want to; but we publish many articles because we believe the subjects to be something which the readers should know and of which they should be informed.

Maybe once a year we try to touch on something like transpersonal psychology. Maybe once a year or oftener, meditative techniques. Perhaps once a year, drugs and psychic phenomena.

Each one of those topics is a field in itself, of course, and we can only sample them for our readers. And that sampling must be able to be understood by someone at a high school senior's reading level. We know our readers pretty well—their education, their social background, their financial status.

I imagine that you would always welcome articles by academic and laboratory parapsychologists.

MARY: Absolutely, but we are realistic in recognizing that few of those men and women wish to publish in a popular journal such as ours for fear of damaging their professional reputations. We get around the parapsychologists' not wanting to be authors for *Fate* by reprinting the material after it has appeared in a respectable journal. We find that they have little or no objection to our using their articles as reprints.

CURT: Except for the American Society for Psychical Research, which is completely unco-operative.

MARY: The British society has always been wonderful to us, but the American society will not permit us to use any of their material.

But getting back to editorial direction, I would like to point out that we have always been cautious with our subject matter and have always avoided sensationalizing it. The very nature of our material is sensational in its implications. We have only tried to do an honest reportorial job.

There is no question, one learns reviewing the marvelous library of the paranormal that a collection of *Fate*'s back issues produces, that the Fullers have been always very circumspect and exceedingly cautious with their potentially sensational subject matter. I can find only one instance in which, editorially speaking, Curt and Mary got behind a specific psychic and aggressively (for them) championed his cause. I am referring to the controversial Chicago sensitive Ted Serios, the psychic photographer who seemingly influences the film of a Polaroid camera and causes it to bear images by means of mental interaction with its sensitive chemicals.

In December 1962, *Fate* ran the first article-length examination of Serios' remarkable talent. The report was written by Pauline Oehler, Vice President, Illinois Society for Psychic Research, and contained Serios' psychic photographs of such landmarks as the south portico of the Chicago Museum of Natural History; the arch over the main entrance to the mosque at Fatehpur Sikri, twenty-three miles from Agra, India; part of the garden of the Taj Mahal; and the United States Capitol.

In many instances, so testified several teams of researchers, Serios had but to think of the building in order to replicate it through psychic means. In most specimens, though, Serios seldom had any idea what images would be found on the film. It seemed as though he but served as a channel for some paranormal process which produced photographs of literally everything from faces to frescoes. In those samples where Serios produced identifiable landmarks, photographic experts stated that the images would had to have been taken with wide-angle lenses or telephoto lenses, at incredibly awkward angles—sometimes at dangerous elevations.

It was through the Pauline Oehler article that prominent parapsychologist Dr. Jule Eisenbud became interested in a thorough laboratory investigation of the phenomenon that was Ted Serios.

In the July 1965 issue, Canadian psychical researcher Allen Spraggett reported on tests that skeptical photographic experts in Toronto imposed upon Serios. Spraggett began his article by stating that "careful research" had convinced Dr. Eisenbud "beyond all possible doubt that Chicago's Ted Serios actually can photograph objects that aren't there."

After witnessing the Toronto tests, Spraggett offered his own assessment of Serios' abilities: "One thing I am sure of: Ted Serios can do the 'impossible' and in doing it he gives one more indication that this universe is vastly more complex than many scientists fancy it to be."

In August 1967 Curt devoted his "I See by the Papers" column to the only formal editorial statement that *Fate* has made in its twenty-five years of existence. The statement, so Fuller wrote, had a dual purpose: "To assess the immense significance of Dr. Jule Eisenbud's book, *The World of Ted Serios,* and to discuss the difficulties of encouraging or conducting responsible research into such an unorthodox subject."

Why did *Fate* consider the research with Ted Serios to be so important?

"The answer is quite obvious," Curtis Fuller wrote: "Ted Serios is a unique one-man laboratory in which all the proof an open-minded investigator needs is contained in one handy package!

"Consider this: When Ted Serios takes a psychic photograph, within 10 seconds before your eyes you have proof of psychokinesis, of telepathy, of clairvoyance, sometimes even of time transference. Here is visual physical evidence. A single Ted Serios photograph taken under controlled conditions is worth 10 years of statistics painfully gathered, carefully extrapolated, because *here it is*—unmistakable, irrefutable. Just try to duplicate it by 'normal' means!

"To us therefore the Ted Serios phenomenon represents in capsule form the mysteries, truths, problems of psychic research and is the avenue to its acceptance by orthodox (and other) scientists.

"Let us go a step farther. If the claims we are making for Ted Serios are true—and indeed if the other claims made by parapsychology are true—then science as we know it today is giving us a false picture of physical reality and of the world in which we live!"

There were, of course, those who believed that they could duplicate Ted Serios' psychic photography by "normal means." Well, perhaps not really *normal* means, because they were employing trickster devices known professionally to them in their work as stage magicians. Serios found himself the target of professional magicians, who sought to debunk him in much the same manner as the prestidigitators seek to expose Uri Geller today. Interestingly, but hardly coincidentally, Serios and Geller became targets for the same principal antagonist, the Amazing Randi.

In the August 1974 issue of *Fate,* Curtis Fuller compiled an article from the correspondence between Dr. Eisenbud and

Randi that should be required reading for anyone who earnestly believes that the replication of psychic phenomena by professional magicians thereby invalidates psychic phenomena. To say, as do the magicians, that to be able to duplicate a paranormal effect by trickery is to prove that a psychic accomplished the manifestation in the same manner is simply not so. A man naked under a laboratory smock, thoroughly searched for any device alien to his natural physical state, yet still able to produce effects ostensibly denied mortals according to the dictates of conventional science, is hardly the same thing as a man fully clothed in evening attire or theatrical costume—every drape, fold, or tuck carefully hiding an extensive array of electronic or other carefully selected paraphernalia—being able to reproduce those same effects.

In our day of scientific wonders, there is nothing that cannot be replicated—or *appear* to be replicated. But just as the most beautifully wrought artificial rose does not negate the reality of real roses, neither does the artificially wrought stage presentation of psychic phenomena negate the reality of real psychic manifestations and occurrences.

Fuller's article, "Dr. Jule Eisenbud vs. the Amazing Randi," documents how, in spite of his vociferous claims to have duplicated, and thereby demolished, Serios' feats of psychic photography, Randi repeatedly ". . . avoided his promise to duplicate Ted's accomplishments and in so doing remained the court favorite of the Establishment and their ill-informed spokesman." Curt says he was motivated to write the article to illustrate ". . . how difficult it is for a psychic or a psychical researcher to build a reputation and how easy it is for those who wish to demolish reputations to gain a national platform."

In the February 1975 issue of *Fate,* the Fullers ran Serios' "Open Letter to the Amazing Randi," in which the much-maligned psychic photographer challenged the Amazing One to duplicate his photographs by "trickery or any other means under controlled conditions," so long as Randi does not bring a psychic person to assist him and agrees that for every test the target will be changed and that every target will be selected at the last minute. At this writing (June 1975) and to my knowledge, the magician has not responded to the challenge issued by the psychic.

You have often been crticized for the sensational nature of some of the advertising which you accept, regardless of how cautious you may be editorially.

CURT: A lot of those same ads are appearing in the New York *Times* book section. In fact, they will run ads which we turn down!

MARY: Curt really feels worse about the advertisements than I do. He received a lot of criticism when he was on the board of Spiritual Frontiers Fellowship. People would nail him for this or that ad, and he would take it personally. He would come home feeling badly about it and ask me to cut the ad. I didn't always do it, however.

CURT: We do have ethical standards for advertising.

MARY: I have reviewed all the ads for *Fate* since the day I opened an issue and saw that we were selling rides to the Moon! After that, I said that I would look at all of the ads as my responsibility.

We don't expect to keep you from wasting your money. We feel that it is your money, and you can do whatever you wish with it. But we do intend that you should not be hurt by anything which we advertise.

We don't allow people to advertise personal consultations where they can come directly to the reader's house. We do permit consultations through the mail, but we don't want people coming to a reader and having him or her apply personal pressures.

We don't run vanity publishing company ads, because we feel they really do take people for their money. They really do not sell the pay-for-publication authors' books. You will regularly find ads for vanity publishers in the New York *Times*.

We just turned down a two-page ad that would have brought in over a thousand dollars, because of its headline: "Learn How to Secretly Control Other Peoples' Minds." Personally, I don't believe such a thing is possible, but I still will not permit such an advertisement in *Fate*.

We won't advertise cures for diseases which we think are well within the domain of medical doctors. Things that are within the nature of home remedies, for such ailments as arthritis, we let by.

Anything I feel is a con game, I squelch at once. I can't say that all of our advertising is great, but it is pretty much harmless.

CURT: I would like to address myself to the philosophical implications of the advertising. Often when people criticize us for some of our ads, I respond by saying that we are very concerned about this matter. I state that we have tried to draw up guidelines upon which everyone might agree. I appeal to them to assist us.

Suppose, for example, the Christian church submitted an ad for *Fate*. With all the claims Christianity makes, how could we possibly fit them into any guidelines which we might draw up for advertisements in *Fate?* We would have to turn that ad down with all the others.

Imagine that ad: Touch the hem of his garment and be healed! Speak to the Son of God! See him walk on water! See him ascend to Heaven upon his death!

What should we do with such an ad? Well, you see my point. Who are we to judge what some of these people can or cannot do?

I feel that we must have the same kind of openness in regard to editorial material. We believe that anything is possible. We believe everything—and nothing. We do not believe that all the answers are in yet.

I think I regard *Fate* as a mystery magazine. Not in the sense of a detective magazine, but that the whole world is full of mysteries, and we are here to report them.

MARY: The whole philosophical concept that the editorial policy of *Fate* has is that we really don't understand the world we live in; therefore, any of these things may be true.

We don't know if it is presumptuous on our part, but we feel that we have contributed to the change in society's attitude toward the subjects in which *Fate* is interested. We feel that we may have helped remove the kook labels from so many things in this field because we were not behaving like lunatics in the beginning years of *Fate*. We are just part of the pattern now, but twenty years ago we were very much alone.

I don't think any fair-minded observer of the psychic scene would argue with that, Mary. At this point, though, I would like to ask if you think it is merely accident that caused you to create Fate *in Chicago?*

MARY: We feel in our bones that Chicago is a kind of center of the country. If you are living in Chicago, you are in contact with the heart of the nation. In Chicago, you *really* know what people are interested in. New York is busy telling the nation what people should be interested in. When you go to New York, you somehow lose touch with people's true pulse and true feelings.

As to why we started *Fate* here, this obviously had to do with the people to whom we were talking. This kind of thing is something that you take in with your pores and with the very air you breathe. The same reasons why Chicago is big in the psychic field are probably the same reasons why *Fate* started here.

I think a reason why the interest in psychic matters seems to be of higher quality in Chicago is that in California, for example, too many people have gone too far out. They have become rather irresponsible in their attitudes and too disorganized. They have gone off on too many tangents. Whereas in Chicago people are pretty well organized and pretty well structured.

And Fate *itself is certainly well structured. You aren't winging off in far-out avenues of metaphysical meanderings.*

CURT: I can't speak for Mary, but when I sit down to write "I See by the Papers," I am continually struck by all the fantastic material that flows into this office. To me, so many amazing things happen. I am perpetually filled with a sense of wonder.

MARY: My sense of wonder doesn't really stand up to three proofreadings, but I really do enjoy working on *Fate*. I would like to mention that it has been lots of fun. It is hard not to be enthusiastic about *Fate*.

—3

A City of "Psych-ins"

I WOULD ONLY PROVOKE a needless argument if I credited any one person or any one group with the original concept of the "psych-in"—a large gathering of psychics, palmists, astrologers, and so forth in a trade-fair atmosphere—but surely few would dispute my stating that Joe and Alexandria East must have been among the first to assemble large numbers of sensitives and practitioners of the occult arts under one roof. Joe and Alexandria are the unofficial directors of The Group, a loosely knit guild of two hundred psychics, who hold their happenings most often at the Lawson Y.M.C.A.

"We send out about two thousand flyers every month," Joe told me. "We spend all our money promoting psychics. We keep our people in the public eye, because that is the only way we can be certain of building crowds for our lectures.

"There is a lot of competition among psychics in Chicago, but we all get along well. We all know each other, and we all help each other. If we have somebody booked for a radio or television show and he can't make it, we can call someone else to fill in right away. And we plug each other constantly."

I asked Joe how active he was in lecturing before his peers. He laughed. "I've been too busy promoting, I guess. This is the tenth year of The Group, and I have only spoken once, and that was to make an announcement."

Rev. Charlotte Zuffante, psychic consultant and healer, whom I met for the first time at John Miller's Midwest Psychic Fair at McCormick Place, April 10–13, 1975, feels that Chicago's finely tuned vibration comes from the sensitives who have gathered there.

"One morning as I was preparing to go to work, I suddenly became very ill. I called my employer and he told me to stay home," Reverend Zuffante said. "I was sitting reading my Bible when a master appeared in the midst of the most beautiful golden light. This is the truth. I could not lie about such a thing. The master stayed about three minutes. It took me nearly forty years of study before this happened to me. Other masters had appeared briefly, but they were none of them like this golden master. When you begin to be led by the hand, you know that you will not have to worry any more.

"I feel that Chicago is a center for these masters to come through. Unseen forces are waiting to manifest!"

In addition to running the Astro-Occult Book Shoppe at 2517 West Seventy-first Street, astrologer Elinora Jaksto pubblishes *Midwest Psychic News,* a monthly newsletter of psychic events in Chicago and the Midwest, and *Chicago Psychic Guide,* a "who's who" listing of Chicago psychics.

"John Miller puts on the big psychic fairs," Elinora, an active member of the Midwest Psychic Fair Association, explained. "He's got hundreds of psychics available from the Chicago area, and he brings in name speakers and demonstrators from all over the nation. But if anyone should want to put on a 'mini-psychic fair,' he can call Irene Diamond on the Northside or myself on the Southside. We can put one together on very short notice, and we have about twenty readers virtually on call for these fairs."

Elinora recalls how people laughed at her when she opened her first occult-astrological-metaphysical bookstore, in 1965.

"Awareness wasn't as high then," she commented. "When I said that interest in psychic matters would burst out in Chicago and that Chicago would become the psychic center, people pooh-poohed my prediction. No longer does the man on the Chicago streets doubt this! Chicago is right now the psychic center of the United States—if not the world. Minneapolis, by the way, is a close second. How interesting that both cities should be midwestern!"

Irene Diamond expressed her opinion that a magnetism peculiar to the Polish people has contributed an important element to the alchemical mixture that has made Chicago North America's most psychic city.

"The Polish people have been led here in great numbers," Irene said. "There has been much suffering in their lives. They have had to work hard and struggle to stay alive. Now is the time for God to bring them forward. He will do this in Chicago."

With proud affirmation, Irene admitted that she was of Polish ancestry. "Chicago will be the central pioneering spirit in the New Age," she continued. "Chicago will help make the New Age harmonious, balanced, peaceful. It is my belief that we have had enough catastrophes. We must now think about perfection and release all the negative vibrations. By denying the negativity, we shall also deny the catastrophes which so many people have predicted as heralding the dawn of the New Age."

I met Marion Kuntz at a Spiritual Frontiers Fellowship conference, and I have since found her to be a wise woman of a solid metaphysical background.

"I think the fact that Chicago is the psychic center of America is what has saved all of us here from what could have been some pretty bad situations," Marion remarked. "While

A City of "Psych-ins"

there have been some potentially dangerous and destructive events occurring in Chicago during the past seven years, there has been a tremendous amount of upliftment at the same time. This is because there are so many people here in Chicago who truly follow the spiritual path.

"It seems to me," Marion went on, "that a great number of 'soul families' have come together in Chicago. Perhaps a number of these may be working in precise ways unknown to themselves. You remember that Edgar Cayce decreed this to be one of the safe parts of the country in the coming earth changes. Perhaps the spiritually disciplined have been centered here in order to be able to spread out if the disasters do take place as predicted.

"I feel that right now we are in the time of Job. Never before have I felt so tested. Other psychics say the same thing. Everything is being thrown at all of us. Everyone that I know is having his or her whole way of life swept out. These are challenges and tests which we can endure, however. We can survive, and we can be strengthened by the experience of testing."

Fate magazine's associate editor and book-review columnist, David Techter, frequently attends psych-ins both as a lecturer and as a reader. Just before we both participated in John Miller's April 1975 psychic fair, I asked Dave how he accounted for the great contemporary interest in such events.

"It is hard to give a definitive answer, Brad," he replied. "There is certainly a discouragement with the traditional systems of value. The Church has lost credence. People are looking around for something different. I don't know if I am so hopeful that I would term this an Age of Aquarius, a new consciousness coming in, for many things look very discouraging to me.

"Actually, I think the phenomenal interest in the psychic, occult, metaphysical field on the part of the average man peaked about two years ago. Where the action is now is within the people in the power structure. The universities are opening up, and the scientists are beginning to take serious recognition of the field. But even more importantly, the interest in this field is moving into the upper-middle class. The lower class has had this interest all along. The very wealthy have always believed in these abilities, and they have been profiting from them. Now psychism is receiving credence because it is moving into the power structure.

"At the same time," Dave continued, "we have our psychical research centers going broke. Even the Society for Psychical Research here in America has said that they may not make their first century. No one has ever figured out how to translate the tremendous interest in the occult and metaphysics into money for research."

I asked Dave for his opinion concerning the popularity of psych-ins in the Chicago area.

"It is very surprising, in one way, to find so much interest in the paranormal in our city. California has an enthusiasm for the occult field largely, I think, because it has retained the 'last frontier' syndrome, where people like to break the old patterns and start over again.

"But Chicago is not a frontier. It is an old, established, and basically conservative community.

"And look not far from us: Peoria and Indianapolis are very psychic communities. Milwaukee has active psychic groups. Minneapolis is growing stronger in the psychic field with each passing year. The Midwest is surprisingly active at the same time that it is basically conservative.

"One thing that has contributed to the high-level activity in Chicago and the whole of Illinois is that Illinois was one of the first states to abolish the old fortunetelling law. There are still some archaic local blue laws, but the story is that former governor Otto Kerner's mother received a very impressive reading from a psychic. His mother then told him that he should get rid of those repressive laws so that her friends could practice their psychism. That may explain why psych-ins are so popular here. There are fewer restrictions here against one's practicing his psychic ability for remuneration."

Kathleen Fry, palmist and past-life reader, is a frequent

participant at Chicago-area psych-ins. Kathleen is certain that there are some very unusual psychic vibrations which have been building up in the Chicago area.

"You know, they talk about the Bermuda Triangle and other such areas around the world," Kathleen began, "but I think we have some kind of 'triangle' over Chicago. It is just as if there is some powerful force trying to come through in Chicago.

"I feel that more and more people are going to become aware of their psychic powers. People are always saying to me, 'I wish I was psychic like you are.' I tell them, 'You are, but you just don't use it!'

"For the nation, 1976 is going to be an important psychic year. We began our national independence in 1776; I believe that 1976 is going to be a year of spiritual rebirth for many Americans."

Chicago is fortunate in having a number of media personalities who are knowledgeable about the psychic field. While most of them maintain an open-minded skepticism toward psychic phenomena, clairvoyance, and the alleged percentage of accuracy claimed by some of the contemporary seers who guest their programs, such men as Ed Schwartz, WIND; Jim Conway, WNUS; Dave Baum, WFLD; Bill Nigut, WLTD; and Mike Edwards, WBBM; give those who are in tune with the "vibes" of Psychic Chicago a fair-minded hearing for their favorite subject. Veteran broadcaster Warren Freiberg has gone so far as to establish a parapsychology foundation in Park Forest.

Each of the above-named media personalities has an enormous personal following. Preparatory to appearing at John Miller's Midwest Psychic Fair, I appeared on several radio and television programs. I stopped counting, after a couple of hundred, the men, women, and school kids who greeted me with: "I heard you the other night on Chicago Schwartz!" "Great rap you had with Jim last night." "Hey, that was a great show you did with Dave Baum!" "I fell asleep listening to you on Mike Edwards, but I stayed awake as long as I could. Did you talk all night?"

On January 10, 1970, I was pleased to be in attendance at what might have been one of the first psych-ins to be held over radio. Bess Krigel, the ebullient Psychic Chicago schoolteacher, was at that time hostess of a Saturday morning program, *ESP with Bess,* over WWCA, Gary, Indiana. Although we have now crossed a state line, the psychic emanations that permeate the Psychic Chicago area pay little heed to man-made geographical demarcations. State chauvinists need not bother to nit-pick. In my definition, Gary is very much a part of Psychic Chicago, for I am speaking of spiritual vibrations, not of civic distinctions.

At that time, I was doing an annual assessment of the predictions of the nation's outstanding seers for *Fate* magazine. Since so many of these prophets were in the Chicago area, Bess called me to suggest they make their predictions during a live broadcast, which I could then duly chronicle.

Joe DeLouise made his on-the-air predictions via a telephone hookup as he packed his suitcase for an out-of-town speaking engagement; and I read Irene Hughes's prognostications, because she was unable to attend due to a previous commitment. Those psychics in attendance for the broadcast were Harold Schroeppel, President of Haly's Psychic Self Improvement; Olof Jonsson, who would later participate in astronaut Edgar Mitchell's moon-to-earth ESP experiment during Apollo 14; Mae Darling; Milton Kramer, well known as the psychic bellman; medium Ruth Zimmerman; and astrologers Dr. Lasca Bogdanova and Mrs. Merle Meyer. Chicago is the city of psych-ins, but I think that Bess may have come up with a "first" in her idea of the psychics broadcasting their predictions for the New Year, together with informative opinions and folksy insight.

Matin Ciani feels that while Chicago manifests a balanced type of energy, its psychic practitioners must be cautious in this time of transition.

"We are living in an age of instant karma; that is what I

A City of "Psych-ins"

call this transition period," Matin said. "I feel that no matter what you do, it seems to manifest either tenfold *for* or tenfold *against*. One must be very careful what he is doing.

"Because of this time of transition, this time of instant karma, event-oriented psychics are having difficulty with accuracy. I, myself," Matin explained, "am an humanistically oriented psychic. I try to seek the pattern with the individual and go into his subconscious.

"But because of this time of constant changing, I feel that some of the best readings which one will receive will come from the newer psychics, young people who have had to roll with the energies. Too many of the old-timers among the psychics are confused by this instant-karma time, and their accuracy is falling.

"Because Chicago emanates a lot of equal balances among the newer energies, we are going to see an exciting type of New Age psychic coming from this city. We are going to see psychics emerging who will accept all of these mysteries as reality, not as esoteric mysticism. Chicago will continue to be the nation's hub of psychic activity into the New Age."

—4

Irene Hughes, the Queen of Psychic Chicago

WHILE IT IS TRUE that I have shared many very meaningful spiritual experiences with Irene Hughes, I suppose I recall most often a time that was both eerie and comedic.

We had been drawn to an estate in a midwestern city to investigate charges that the place was haunted. Numerous witnesses, including police officers in patrol cars, had observed such ghostly phenomena as the materialization of a glowing, human-shaped thing.

Our psychic safari arrived on the scene the night before we were scheduled to meet with the caretaker and a number of police officers, who would accompany us on a tour of the grounds and the ancient, crumbling mansion. Glenn McWane, my investigative associate, pointed the nose of the station wagon down the tree-draped lane of the old estate and shut off the lights. Right on cue, with a timing that would be envied by a Hollywood production, we watched a glowing, man-shaped thing, perhaps twenty yards in front of us, move across the lane and glide toward the old house.

A chain across the driveway prevented us from driving closer. Glenn and I began to open our car doors, but Irene suddenly cautioned us against a closer investigation on that night.

The next evening, we were parked in front of the moldering manse. Glenn and I were in the front seat, a police officer between us. Irene, two journalists, and a friend were in the back. The thickly matted tree branches and unrestrained vegetation on the unkempt grounds prevented any external light source from permeating the area near us on that moonless night.

Then, directly in front of the automobile's hood, we saw what appeared to be a bit of sparkling, illuminated mist beginning to swirl like animated moonbeams.

The police officer made a strange noise in his throat as he took notice of the eerie bit of business going on outside. Glenn and I knew that the officer would attempt to keep his professional cool, so we decided to try some one-upmanship.

The glowing stuff was becoming much less amorphous and much more clearly defined. Beads of sweat were popping out along the policeman's forehead. "There seems to be something forming in front of the car," he said in a hoarse whisper.

"Yes," I agreed, "there certainly does seem to be something there all right."

"Well, what the hell is it!" he shouted, breaking his professional aloofness, displaying his humanity in the same sort of plaintive wail that has issued from men's throats ever since the species became intelligent enough to observe such phenomena and to wonder about their origin.

That was when Irene took over. Her psyche had a much finer tuning mechanism than did ours. She was able to see features and to describe what she saw about the glowing, man-shaped thing precisely enough to gain shocks of recognition from the caretaker.

Half-heard, soft whispers floated about us on the hot summer's darkness. Some of us caught a word here, a phrase there, but Irene was able to understand and to relay messages, which again made the caretaker gasp in wonder. She was picking up names, dates, particularly important events in the history of the decaying estate.

Irene Hughes, seer, clairvoyant, mystic, made lasting converts to the validity of psi abilities on that most interesting night on our psychic safari.

In this book, I have named Irene Hughes the Queen of Psychic Chicago. In my opinion, Irene has earned this title by merit of the incredibly wide range of her psychic abilities; the regal, professional manner in which she conducts herself on all occasions; and by virtue of her steady, high-quality propagandizing on behalf of psychism through her books, newspaper columns, radio shows, lecture programs, weekend retreats, and television appearances. In addition to the above activities, Irene maintains The Golden Path, wherein one might enroll for instruction in psychic and spiritual development. And she has not neglected her physical humanhood. Irene has mothered four children through the vicissitudes of maturation in twentieth-century America, and now she and her husband, Bill, are grandparents.

Irene Hughes first achieved national prominence when she predicted the exact dates for the Chicago area's three major blizzards during January and February of 1967. From that foreseen event on, the telephones in her office of The Golden Path have not stopped jangling with requests for psychic guidance from law-enforcement officers, troubled housewives, harried businessmen, professional football players, media celebrities, and U.S. senators.

Irene issues dozens of predictions each year, many in her newspaper columns, several "live" over the broadcast media, and the obligatory number in annual prediction features for various print media. Because her innate sense of orderliness demands it, Irene's predictions are always announced well in advance of the foreseen event. She never resorts to the shaky and suspect device of claiming to have "told a friend" about a dramatic event after it has already come into realization. Because she scrupulously issues her prophetic pronouncements well before the events have moved into place on the conventional time cycle, Irene presents a solid roadblock to the skeptic.

At the same time, because she makes so many predictions, it is admittedly difficult to assess her precise degree of accuracy. Although her prophecies are much more specific than those of many of her peers, the question of interpretation does enter into a rigid evaluation of her prophetic prowess. I still study Irene's yearly predictions with some degree of thoroughness, but there was a four-year period, 1968–72, when I meticulously compiled evidential data for her hits and misses. At that time, in my opinion I had to give her at least 80 per cent accuracy.

Irene Hughes never photographs as attractive as she is in life. There is a lively twinkle in her eye that I have never seen a camera quite capture. She carries herself like the model she once was, and she is justly proud of the journalism awards she has received, which proves that she has creativity and brains in addition to the talent of psychism.

Irene has retained a good many of the speech patterns of the rural Tennessee area in which she was born and reared. Although she is always extremely circumspect in her public behavior, there is strangely just a hint of the mildly flirtatious southern belle about Irene. Roll the years back with our Magic Time Machine, and I can visualize her sparkling eyes winking over a lace fan at a fancy ball on her father's plantation.

In this life, however, Irene hardly came from a plantation background. She was one of the twelve children of Easter Bell and Joe Finger; and from the time she was nine until she was fifteen she milked cows, hoed cotton, cut sugar cane, and chopped wood, doing her part to keep enough food in their little four-room cabin.

Irene started having "feelings" when she was but four years old. Easter Bell, who was half Cherokee, and Joe, a tall Scots-English woodsman, were tuned in enough with the vibrations of the Earth Mother so that they never laughed at their child. Although survival occupied too much of the family's time for them to permit Irene to sit around and have visions all day, they did take heed when the child told them when it would rain and when the cotton should be picked.

I have always been fascinated with Irene's recounting of the visit of the "wee people" who approached her when she was very young. Irene remembers especially the fairy queen, no larger than herself, who never stopped smiling, and whose clothing was nothing more than wisps and puffs of some kind of shiny material. The queen was blond, just as Irene was, and the little girl knew that she had always known that the tiny queen was somewhere around her.

Before the fairy queen left Irene, she promised the girl a new doll and a string of beads—treasures that seemed impossible dreams to a child aware of her family's financial circumstances. But more important by far than the material gifts, Irene was told that she had the "ability to feel many strange and wonderful things."

Little Irene was a blonde in a family of dark-complexioned brunettes. Since earliest childhood, she had been nicknamed "Queenie." Was the fairy queen Irene's own Anima, a projection of the intuitive aspect of her personality? Or was the little lady a visiting entity from some other realm of being? She was somehow interested in the child Irene's future development.

In his *Autobiographical Writings,* Hermann Hesse recalls his own mysterious companion entity: ". . . I do not know when I saw him for the first time: I think he was always there, that he came into the world with me. The little man was a tiny, gray, shadowy being, a spirit or goblin, angel or demon, who at times walked in front of me in my dreams as well as during my waking hours, and whom I had to obey, more than my father, more than my mother, more than reason, yes, often more than fear."

Irene Hughes, Queen of Psychic Chicago

When Irene was fifteen, she made her confession of faith to a Baptist minister who was serving in a Church of the Nazarene. As she stood before the altar, she felt as if she had been immersed in a huge body of water, and that as the water flowed off her, a fountain manifested within her, actually taking the place of her heart. She knew that it was a fountain of joy, and she is aware of that fountain within her to this day. It is one reason why she feels compassion for other people.

"I have learned in the years after to really listen and to really experience the tremendous ecstasy and the calming peace within me," Irene said. "I believe that this calm and peace is something that everyone might acquire if he prepares himself through prayer and study. He must learn that it is not enough to *ask* for something when he prays. He must *affirm* that it is so. Affirmation shows faith, and in faith comes an overwhelming experience of knowing. I feel that man, in small groups or by himself, is becoming more aware that God is within him and not in some far-distant heaven, and that he does not have to seek Him in strange places, but that he can find Him where He really is."

Although Irene belongs to no formal church today, she respects all faiths, all pathways to God.

Once when we were discussing such things as "belief," "visualization," and "affirmation," Irene told me that, to her, belief is mental visualization. To believe is to draw a mental blueprint. When one has accomplished that, he has eliminated the word "impossible" from his thinking. Once one has visualized his goal in his mind, athough it may not yet be manifested in reality, he has come to know that the goal is possible to attain.

It may be that the little fairy queen still walks with Irene on some shadowy level, just as Hesse's little man remained with him; but after a severe illness, in June 1961, she received a spirit teacher whose actual name she may not yet reveal. For purposes of discussion, she has called him "Kaygee." In his earth-plane existence he had been a marvelous Oriental gentleman who had spent his entire life fighting for the living truth in the slums of his nation.

Early in his materializations, the entity provided Irene with an astonishing amount of veridical evidence to prove that he was who he claimed to be. Kaygee gave Irene the name of his daughter, who at that time was in the United States studying at Cornell University. Irene wrote to her, and she verified that her father had been one of the greatest Japanese Christians of the century, and that he had died in April 1961. The fact that the name and address the entity had given her had proved to be correct seemed to Irene to be most evidential of Kaygee's survival after death. She accepted the reality of his spirit coming to work through her.

One evening, Irene, my wife Marilyn, a few close friends, and I were seated on the floor about a flickering candle. We were not actually holding a séance as much as we were engaged in meditation. My attention, though, was drawn to Irene, and it seemed obvious that she was going into trance.

I must make mention of the fact that Irene seldom employs the trance state in her work. She is essentially a mental medium, not a trance medium.

But tonight Irene was apparently going to slip into an exception to her rule. Others in the circle had begun to notice what was happening, and soon everyone's attention was directed to Irene.

Then her mannerisms suddenly altered, and her very appearance seemed to be transformed. An authoritative voice issued from her throat, providing the circle with brief lessons of profound metaphysical instruction.

The visitation proved to be a brief one. Irene's familiar facial expression returned along with her full consciousness.

"It was Kaygee," I said softly. We had all felt privileged to be present during one of the rare occasions when Irene completely surrendered her physical vehicle to become a channel for the spirit of Kaygee.

Irene nodded her verification. It was apparent that she had had no presentiment that such a visitation would occur that night.

Irene believes that Kaygee chose her as a channel because the entity assessed her to be so physically, emotionally, and psychically constructed that he would be able to work well through her. She considers herself honored to have been chosen as the vehicle by which Kaygee might manifest at least certain aspects of his work.

Since Irene most often receives psychic impressions, that is, communications, from the minds of those still on the earth plane, such as her clients who visit The Golden Path, I once asked her how she was able to distinguish between simple telepathy and communication from the dimensions of spirit.

"I really don't have a problem in this regard, Brad," she replied. "When I am quiet, completely relaxed, deep in meditation, either alone at home or in a prayer circle, I experience a tingling sensation, similar to a chill, first on my right ankle, then on my left. Eventually, this tingling spreads to cover my entire body. It is almost as though a soft, silken skin has been pulled glove-tight over me. It is not an uncomfortable feeling. I actually find it to be quite soothing, and by now I am on my way to that golden flow of consciousness that is the spirit plane. I am still in semi-trance, though. If I were in full trance, I would not be able to recall a single thing."

With Irene's permission, I have placed my hands upon her own while she is in this state. I have always found them to be extremely cold.

"That is because I have become as one with the spirit plane," she explained. "I grow cold as death itself, but I am not at all uncomfortable. My entire body, though, has been transformed so that it is not unlike one great sense organ, alert to every motion, every nuance of feeling, every minute aspect of cosmic magnificence. Although my body may feel cold to you, I am now enveloped in an exquisite warmth. I am surrounded by a magnificent light."

It is at that point that Irene becomes aware of her spirit teacher, Kaygee. He waves his hand, ushering those of the spirit plane forward so that those who wish might speak to friends and relatives through the channel of the medium.

"Although at that state of consciousness I am a wide-open channel," Irene said, "the messages come so quickly that I simply cannot relay them fast enough. Consequently, I fear that many messages may be incomplete, and sometimes downright confusing to the recipient."

Irene has often said that spirit guests appear just as they did when they mainfested upon the earth plane. Often they hold an object that they owned in the physical state of existence so that the medium may more readily identify them to the loved ones who are waiting to hear from them.

"Telepathy has quite a different feeling from spirit communication," Irene went on to clarify. "My recognition of thought sources is instant and certain. I am always aware when the communicator of a certain thought is among the living or when he is in spirit."

There was a most dramatic situation, in early October of 1970, that called upon every ounce of Irene Hughes's psychic reserves and her ability to distinguish keenly the source of thoughts, emotions, and planes of existence.

On October 5, 1970, Senior British Trade Commissioner James Richard (Jasper) Cross was snatched from his Montreal residence by abductors who pretended to be delivering a birthday gift for him.

Shortly after the kidnaping, representatives of the *Front de Liberation Quebecois* (FLQ) contacted government authorities through a local radio station and admitted that members of their organization had carried out the abduction. For the safe return of the diplomat, the FLQ demanded the release of twenty-three persons being held in Canadian jails as "political prisoners."

On October 10, a mere five days after Cross's abduction, an FLQ group calling itself the Chenier Cell kidnapped Quebec Labor Minister Pierre Laporte. They demanded the same ransom as for Cross, and threatened the life of their victim. The kidnaping of Laporte created more of a stir among French-speaking Canadians, because the Labor Minister was the senior cabinet minister in the Quebec Government, second only to Premier Robert Bourassa. Cross, on the other hand, was a ranking member among what the separatists call *Les Anglais* (The English).

On Wednesday afternoon, October 14, hoping to obtain some kind of lead in the kidnapings, Canadian broadcast journalist Robert Cummings telephoned Irene Hughes. The conversation that followed was tape-recorded at the same time it was aired live on Cummings' *Afterthought* show over CJCI, Prince George, British Columbia.

Cummings spent less than two minutes explaining to Irene why he was calling; then, after pointing out to his listeners that he had not allowed the psychic adequate time for meditation, he asked her to give her psychic impressions of the Cross and Laporte kidnapings. An abbreviated transcript of that broadcast follows.

IRENE HUGHES: With the first gentleman [Cross], I feel that no physical harm will come to him. However, I feel there *will be* physical harm to the second.

ROBERT CUMMINGS: Now, the newspapers in Chicago are keeping you informed, eh?

IRENE: I've not read the papers today, so I don't know what has happened up to this point.

CUMMINGS: So you feel the British diplomat, Cross, will not be harmed but you fear for Laporte, the cabinet minister from Quebec?

IRENE: Yes, this is true.

CUMMINGS: Can you get a psychic impression as to the arrest of the FLQ responsible for the kidnaping of these two?

IRENE: Well, it's my impression that it may be two to three months, Bob. But I feel that within that time an arrest will come. Actually, I would pinpoint the sixth of November of this year. I said two or three months, but I feel some very striking and unusual news may come on the sixth of November.

CUMMINGS: What do you see for Laporte? Do you see his death?

IRENE: I hesitate very much to make such a prediction as this.

CUMMINGS: But you feel his life is in more serious jeopardy than Cross's?

IRENE: Yes, I do.

CUMMINGS: In other words, Cross has a chance for release, as far as you are concerned?

IRENE: I feel so, yes.

CUMMINGS: Where do you feel these people [FLQ] are hiding out with their victims?

IRENE: I feel they're not far from the original scene.

CUMMINGS: That being Montreal. You feel they're still in the country, still in the province? You already mentioned capture is some weeks away. You don't feel it may be imminent?

IRENE: Well, the news coming out around November 6 may indicate that one of them has been caught or that they have a tremendous lead. . . .

On October 16 the federal government, invoking the War Measures Act, placed all of Canada under martial law. This emergency measure provided the police and other authorities with complete powers of arrest and the right to invade privacy. In the first forty-eight hours, more than three hundred persons were arrested.

Then—on Saturday, October 17—the FLQ kidnapers of Pierre Laporte used a Montreal radio station to tell police that Quebec's Labor Minister had been assassinated. Authorities would find Laporte's body in the trunk of a green Chevrolet at the military base in a section of Montreal known as St. Hubert. The discovery of Laporte's strangled and stabbed corpse set off an angry backlash among conservative Canadians.

Robert Cummings again telephoned Irene Hughes, on the morning of October 18. She had been trying to reach him at the same time to discuss the tragic accuracy of her psychic impression about Pierre Laporte's death.

Here are portions of the second conference between Cummings in Prince George and Mrs. Hughes in Chicago.

IRENE HUGHES: I had the very strangest feeling that I

should say to you that a green car was involved, and I didn't, and I notice that it said in the news that Laporte's body was found in a green car. I was shocked.

ROBERT CUMMINGS: What about Mr. Cross? You indicated to me that he would be released. How do you feel about this now in the light of Laporte's death and the mystery surrounding Cross and the fact that he hasn't turned up?

IRENE: I feel that he is still alive, and I get the impression now that if the authorities offered more money, above and beyond that which has been requested by the FLQ, this man's life might be spared. I feel that he is alive but that he may be ill and very weak.

CUMMINGS: Where is he?

IRENE: I will say five miles northwest of Montreal. It seems that the place he is in is about three stories high. I feel that it is red brick, a kind of old place, and it actually could be an apartment building.

I feel that he is being held under guard, and it is very strange but I see two women involved in that same group. It may be that one of them is taking care of him as far as nursing care is concerned. . . .

. . . It is my impression that some major changes are coming about in your police force . . . to create a different type of protection, but I don't know what this is.

They will not hurt Cross, because they will defeat their own purposes if they do.

CUMMINGS: What was the purpose with Laporte? Do you see Laporte meaning something more to the FLQ in their cause than Cross does?

IRENE: I feel that Laporte was more important to them in their activities than Mr. Cross. The feeling came to me that he [Laporte] had more power involving their personal lives than [Cross].

I have the feeling that [Cross] is in a bed, that he is in bed clothes or not wearing very much. . . . I feel that he has lost weight, and he looks to me rather thin. I do not remember pictures of this man or what he looks like. . . . I had the feeling of intravenous feeding, but I am wondering if something has not been given to him to keep him in an unconscious state or to be unaware of where he is.

CUMMINGS: What do you see particularly next?

IRENE: It could be because of explosions, but I see a huge fire. This may divert attention so [the FLQ] can create other problems.

CUMMINGS: Do you see these fires in government buildings?

IRENE: Yes and in one hospital. [On November 5, 1970, in Montreal seventeen persons died in a major fire in a geriatric hospital.]

In view of the accuracy of Mrs. Hughes's predictions of October 14 and the potential usefulness of the new information, Cummings decided to contact the authorities. He was urged to continue probing for more clues from the Chicago seeress, but the authorities also advised him to discontinue broadcasting his conversations with Mrs. Hughes and to halt the distribution of the special radio programs he had been developing from these interviews.

Cummings made four additional tapes in October, on the eighteenth (during which Mrs. Hughes provided police references from the Cook County Sheriff's Office), the nineteenth, the twentieth, and the twenty-first. Cummings recorded these conversations with the psychic and filed them for future release, then saw to it that transcripts and duplicate tapes were delivered to the authorities as soon as they were completed. None of the information contained on these tapes was made public until the authorities granted clearance, on October 28. Then Cummings prepared a two-part radio program and aired it first over CJCI, on November 6.

On that same date, Irene Hughes's predictions that one of the kidnapers would be arrested on November 6 and that a "tremendous lead" would develop were realized when police apprehended Bernard Lortie in Montreal West. Brought before an inquest on November 7, Lortie confessed to his participation with three others in the abduction of Pierre Laporte. Lortie named his associates as Paul and Jacques Rose and Francis Simard, and these men were arrested early in January 1971 in a Côte St. Luc farmhouse, near Montreal.

Also on November 6, the authorities revealed they had authenticated a recent photo of James Cross along with his signature, which had been received from the FLQ. The photo showed the British trade commissioner seated on a box of explosives playing cards.

Cummings and his associates at CJCI noticed, too, that Mrs. Hughes's prediction of "major changes coming about in your police force . . . to create a different type of protection" had been fulfilled on November 2, when the federal government introduced a bill in the legislature to replace the War Measures Act with a new law authorizing stepped-up police action during times of local crises.

The tapes made on October 19 and 20 reiterated many of the same points Irene had covered in the conversations of the fourteenth and the eighteenth. Here are some interesting exchanges from Cummings' discussion with Mrs. Hughes on October 21 at 9:30 P.M.

ROBERT CUMMINGS: Have you read the latest developments in the paper?

IRENE HUGHES: I heard only about the way Mr. Laporte died, by strangling.

CUMMINGS: Yes, and I recall that you indicated stabbing. He was also stabbed. I argued with you earlier and said that he had been shot, because the early reports out of Montreal had said so. However, the reports were wrong, and your impressions were apparently right. Irene, what about Cross? Do you feel at this moment that he is still alive?

IRENE: I still feel that he is. . . .

CUMMINGS: It seems your indication of Cuban involvement was right. A newspaper story was published tonight about the authorities' suspicions that many of [the FLQ] are actually trained in Cuba.

Three days after Bernard Lortie's arrest and the subsequent occurrences on November 6—the date Mrs. Hughes had foreseen as a day of "striking and unusual" developments in the case—Cummings telephoned her again.

IRENE HUGHES: I've deliberately not read the newspapers here. This can be [attested] only by my family, but I didn't want anything to interfere with my own psychic impressions. I feel that Mr. Cross is still alive, and it is my impression that he will not be assassinated.

. . . [I see] some major action concerning him or some major news concerning him, and it may be that there will be other demands for his release before he will be released.

The November 9 telephone conference was the last in the series of conversations between Cummings and Irene Hughes in connection with the Canadian FLQ crisis.

Then, on December 3, 1970, the international press published the news of Cross's release.

For fifty-nine days, the British diplomat had seen no sun from his three-story brick prison on Des Recollets Street in a northern suburb of Montreal. A week before his release, the police had become certain that Cross was inside the house and had begun to set up a "semivisible" ring of police officers around the area so the FLQ might know they had no exit and must negotiate. At last someone tossed a message out of the dwelling, and government representatives parleyed with the terrorists. After an agreement had been reached, the kidnapers handed Cross over to Cuban diplomats, then boarded a Canadian military plane headed for Cuba. Only when the plane had landed was Cross finally freed. Prime Minister Trudeau described the incident as a nightmare that had passed into history.

"From the first interview," Robert Cummings told me, "Irene Hughes was firm about her psychic impression of the eventual release of James Cross. Television and radio news reports throughout the day of December 3 referred to the developments of that day as the 'final chapter in a most incredible drama.' It was, however, an incredible drama that had had its closing chapter 'written' on the air coast to coast by Irene Hughes three weeks prior to the actual events.

"My mind almost boggles when I consider the remarkable accuracy and detail of Irene's many psychic evaluations concerning this case," Cummings went on. "There were predictions of major consequence, such as the events of November 6 and Cross's release, her accurate description of the Laporte kidnapers' automobile and the three-story brick duplex northwest of Montreal where Cross was held. Irene Hughes had told me and the authorities and the Canadian public all that and much more since October 14. Undoubtedly, this endeavor represents an impressive documentation of ESP at work in a 'now' manner in modern history."

It requires rigid discipline to develop one's psychic abilities to the extent where one can precisely tune in on events transpiring thousands of miles distant. Irene Hughes believes that meditation and concentration are essential to success in the psychic field.

"Don't concentrate so hard that you become upset," she advises. "The student only creates problems for himself when he or she tries too hard to make the mind a blank. As soon as you start to worry because all those extraneous thoughts have not been eliminated from your mind, that is when your head will really start to jam up with crazy impressions. Read some inspirational literature just before your meditation period. Always remember to channel, not force, your thoughts."

—5

Deon Frey—High Priestess of the Tarot

IN DECEMBER 1974 I underwent a visionary experience of an intensely personal, but extremely revelatory, nature. Suffice it to say at this time that the material received will most certainly be expressed in a future written work, but within a few days of my multidimensional contact I received a telephone call from Deon Frey in Chicago. It is typical of the strong bond my family and I have with this remarkable woman that she had "tuned in" on the entire experience and called to discuss what she interpreted as my "higher-plane initiation."

Our first meeting had not begun very harmoniously, however; and I have often mused about the comedy-of-errors circumstances under which we met.

It was in April 1969. I was in Chicago promoting one of my books, and a friend of mine, Rosemarie "Bud" Stewart, was raving about this fantastic Tarot-card reader she had met. She insisted that I find time to go over to the Occult Book Store, on North State Street, where she was working, and arrange for a personal reading.

I at last succumbed to Bud's sales pitch and told her to call Deon and arrange a sitting.

What I did not learn until several years later was that in her excitement and her eagerness to bring two friends together, Bud came on a bit too strong to Deon, who at that time was working a full day as a telephone operator at a Chicago hotel, then filling in at the bookstore to help vacationing friends. To confuse matters even further, Deon was moving apartments that day and was in the midst of domestic upheaval. The one bright spot was that that same chaotic day happened to be her birthday, and a friend had promised to take her to dinner if she could get off work early enough to mesh with his busy schedule.

And that was the night that Bud Stewart chose to call to *tell* Deon that she simply *must* give Brad Steiger a reading.

Unaware of Deon's pique at being prevailed upon at closing time in the bookstore, moving day at her apartment, and the postponing of her birthday dinner, I walked into the Occult Book Store to meet a tall, redheaded woman with rather unfriendly fire in her eyes. By that time in my investigative career, I was used to encountering all kinds of mediums and psychics, so I merely assumed that a rather stern demeanor was simply part of Deon's image—sort of a "sit before me humble client and hear the direct words from the Oracle" approach, which certain mediums seem fond of employing to establish what they consider to be the proper distance between them and their clientele.

We walked back to a small room literally swathed in beaded curtains. I almost chuckled at the stereotypical décor, but I solemnly seated myself opposite Deon at a small, round table.

She pushed back a strand of red hair, began shuffling the deck, then looked up at me and permitted a smile to break her former gruff façade. She tipped her head back and laughed softly at some private joke.

I smiled nervously, wondering if the cards were about to reveal me as the principal character in some vast, cosmic comedy.

I suppose I sensed then, on one level, what I would not know consciously for several years. Deon had established a *rapport* with a deeper level of my essential self, and she knew that before her sat a new friend, not a demanding boor. The mental barrier between us had been shattered, and Deon set about giving me one of the most evidential readings that I have ever received from a professional psychic-sensitive.

As her fingers deftly turned the cards of her small Tarot deck and her psyche tuned in on multidimensional wavelengths, Deon correctly told me that I would travel to New England within two weeks to visit a friend named Bill. She gave the month of my birth and stated that I was Aquarian-Piscean (February 19) married to a Gemini. She described each of my children with his or her peculiar identifying characteristic. She told of my father's recent heart attack. She very accurately described my wife and correctly said that Marilyn had not accompanied me on the Chicago trip because she had elected to stay home to paint the basement.

And she went on and on, becoming more intimate in her revelations, casting farther into the future, suddenly delving deep in my childhood.

The reading terminated with my joining Deon's birthday celebration at her favorite Greek restaurant. In a matter of hours we had become fast friends.

Deon was baptized in the Christian church and reared a Baptist. She took her faith very seriously. Although she has since left that church affiliation, Deon has always tried to emphasize the spiritual in her work.

"I've never wanted to be just a fortuneteller, someone who just sits and reads the cards for people," Deon has often told me. "To me, being a psychic has to be more than simply picking up things on the earth plane. I must try to reach upward for more-meaningful, spiritual truths."

Marilyn and I know from firsthand experience that one of the higher-level manifestations that interests Deon is healing.

In August 1969, a cyst suddenly appeared on Marilyn's throat after a period of rather severe inflammation. Although the doctors said that it was nothing serious, they recommended minor surgery to remove the unsightly lump, which was about the size of a small egg and protruded from Marilyn's throat as if she had an Adam's apple.

A few days before Marilyn was to report to her doctor's office, Deon and a friend stopped by our home in Highland Park. At this point in our married life, Marilyn believed more in me than in my beliefs, and she was rather closed toward the whole concept of unconventional healing.

In spite of her protests, Deon placed Marilyn in an upright chair, and she and her friend began to work on her.

Marilyn squirmed uneasily. "This really can't help," she said, protesting what she must have regarded as some primitive bit of superstitious atavism. "I appreciate what you want to do for me, but seriously, it doesn't hurt all that much. The doctor will soon . . ."

Marilyn became quiet. Something was happening.

The healers had been placing their hands on Marilyn, praying. Now Deon stepped in front of Marilyn and began to make light stroking motions on her throat. Deon raised her fingers above Marilyn's flesh, but continued the stroking movements as she moved her hands higher.

Amazingly, the lump began to move, following the beckoning fingers. The out-of-place Adam's apple kept traveling until it reached the tip of Marilyn's chin—then it vanished!

Marilyn felt her throat in complete bewilderment. "It . . . it's gone," she managed. "The lump is completely gone!"

The demonstration was most impressive. Healing is among the most beautiful acts of human sharing on our troubled planet. All sincere practitioners, from medical doctors to chiropractors, from nutritionists to neurosurgeons, from medicine men to faith healers, have their part to play in alleviating human suffering.

One must be cautious. One must not be gullible, but there is a place for the unconventional, as well as the conventional, in healing. Healing is a channeling of the love energy, an art of the soul as much as a science of the body.

"I experienced my first conscious trance when I was fifteen years old," Deon once told us. "I was a student librarian at Wayne City High. I walked out the door in a trance state, across the street to our home, and into the room where my father lay dead. My cousin entered the school by a side door and told my teacher to send me home because my father had just passed away. She was amazed when she learned that I already had left the building.

"Eternal life was proved to me that very night," Deon recalled. "I was awakened by my father scratching on a screen beside my bed. My father had not been a churchgoer and had not been a believing man. 'You were right, Deon,' he told me. 'If I live, all these people live.'

"Father said he was sorry he had had to leave me so abruptly, especially since because of his death I would never again be able to attend public school. But he did say he would see that I received a different kind of education.

"A year later I moved to Chicago, and my sister Vivian introduced me to Eleanor Dunne, a spiritual medium. During the meeting, an image of my father appeared to me and I understood at once what he had meant by a 'different kind of education.'"

Deon became a member of the National Spiritualist Association and minister of the First Roseland Spiritualist Church. She no longer serves as pastor but maintains her role of teacher through Deon's Psychic Research Center, Box No. 3845, Merchandise Mart.

One of the more interesting experiments in which Deon has participated concerned the identification of objects within a nest of boxes.

"This was in March 1961," Deon said. "Wilbur Smart, who was a member of Spiritual Frontiers Fellowship, first came to me for a consultation. He was impressed with my abilities and asked me to participate in an experiment with a psychical-research study group in London.

"They sent him a large box containing five or six smaller boxes, each wrapped individually. He scheduled this experiment by London time so that the group over there could be sitting at the same time in order to send me vibratory impulses.

"After I was in trance, Wilbur broke the seal on the large box and handed the smaller boxes to me one by one. Wilbur taped my impressions of each box, allowed me to come out of trance, then took his tape recorder and the boxes home with him. He returned the boxes to London unopened.

"I personally never heard the tape, but after London replied I did receive confirmation from Wilbur as to what each of the boxes had contained. If I remember correctly, the boxes were filled with things like locks of hair, pictures, coins. Over all, they gave me a grade of 90 per cent accuracy."

Two weeks later, Wilbur Smart asked Deon if she would participate in another experiment with the British group. Once again Deon went into trance in her room at First Roseland Spiritualist Church while the Londoners sat in their own séance circle. The purpose of this particular experiment was to see if Deon could move an object in the London séance room through long-distance psychokinesis or—depending on one's point of view—the projection of her spirit guide. The experiment was judged successful when either Dr. Speidel, her guide, or Deon's psychokinetic energy moved a large mirror that was hanging over a fireplace just above the heads of the London séance circle.

"The sitters in London attested to the moving of the mirror, which was quite a surprise to me," Deon said. "Wilbur was very secretive about things I did in trance to see if I would mention them in my conscious state."

According to Deon, Dr. Richard Speidel appeared for the first time at her beside one night in 1942. He was of sober mien, dressed formally in a black coat with a black bow tie.

"Will I do?" he asked the startled young woman.

"Will you do for what?" Deon asked with her customary directness and attempting to hide her fear.

"I have been sent to be your guide, your teacher," the entity told her.

Deon has been a part of the psychic world since the age of five. "Lily of the Valley was one of my earlier guides," Deon told me. "And from 1950 to about 1953, Dr. Thomas was my principal guide. He used to whistle for attention. Several people heard his whistle come from a source independent of me, the medium.

"My sister Vivian was an excellent independent voice medium, and the voices of those on the other side would sound from a corner of the ceiling and from distances greatly removed from either her physical body or my own."

Although Deon accepts the reality of Dr. Richard Speidel as an entity independent of her own psyche, she has been able to retain a certain objectivity in regard to her mediumship.

"I wonder sometimes if I really am picking up thought forms from sitters in the séance circle rather than seeing the actual etheric images of those who have passed over," she once admitted. "Or could it be that in trance I somehow travel to another plane of existence and there communicate with entities, rather than that they come back to the earth plane? Can it be that I am only a glorified relay station for vibratory forces?"

It is typical of Deon that she is always asking questions of her preternatural abilities. This is good, for when we are dealing with séances, spirit manifestations, and physical materializations, there is no dogma yet realized that can provide all the answers.

During one séance I attended with Deon serving as the medium, a large, slightly illuminated blob with a rather bright nucleus appeared near the ceiling directly over the reclining medium. A young man, in a voice warped by gasps and sobs, greeted his deceased father. One sitter beheld a grandmother; another a departed friend. I could discern only what appeared to me to be a strange, glowing, jellyfish-shaped thing.

Once during a séance in our home, Deon went into trance,

and at the same time, described the process step by step for the information of those in attendance.

"Okay, I'll face east. . . . I just lie down in the center [of the couch], place my hands at my side. My mind goes in about a thousand different directions. I just lie flat, see?

[In a hoarse voice] "See, they've already started taking my voice, and I'm not even in it yet." [Addressing the group] "Be sure you're relaxed, too. They might want to use you. Now remember, even though I'm here in trance, it is possible for me to walk, move, or whatever they want to do with me.

"If they move me around, I'll go anywhere without touching anything. You don't call me Deon from now on. You can either call me 'one' or 'the medium.' Call me that throughout the séance. Whoever you talk to [referring to entities from the other side] will probably give you their names. However, if they don't, you just talk anyway and try to find out who they are and give them the same courtesy you would if anyone entered your home and wanted to talk to you.

"My body usually gets cold. Last night I got so cold, people thought I was dying. I might act out the part of a spirit, too. So I never know what they're going to do, and I can't promise anything. All I do is lie here and see what happens. . . . I can feel my chest getting heavy. . . . At this point I can feel a terrific vibration in my hands and body.

"It is important to me that you do not keep silent. You must talk among yourselves and create the voice. It is important to him [her spirit guide]. . . . If you are able to see something or feel something or are aware of something that is happening is the room, please talk about it. The louder your voices are, the better the vibrations will be.

[After a few moments, Dr. Richard Speidel, Deon's principal guide, came through.] "Good evening, friends. I am very happy to greet you tonight and work with you in this manner. . . . Always be looking to see what may take place around the medium's face, even though you may become engrossed in conversation. Also keep working with me. Do not let the medium's voice go back to low tone. As you keep talking to it, it will keep talking to you. Do you understand? This is Dr. Richard Speidel, and I work with her in this manner in order to open up the séance and to talk with you."

"I know that I know," Deon once answered when I questioned her regarding the source of a bit of paranormally acquired information she had passed along to me. "I believe that the creative God force works through us at all times. This God force is not always tapped, but it may be used by us. As we use it, we enable it to grow within ourselves and around us."

Another time, Deon described for me a revelatory experience she had undergone:

"The light seemed to be emanating from one corner of the room, and I could almost make out a form. The color was indescribable. It had edges of violet hue, but it was crystal white, or mother-of-pearl, and so bright that it could almost blind me.

"I had a feeling of oneness with it, a unity. It was like being one with everything all at once. The only way I could describe it to myself afterward when I thought of it was like I was water in a sponge. I just became suddenly drawn into it. It was like a love that one really can't understand from the earth plane, because it's such a spiritual envelopment. You want to stay. You don't want to return. You don't want to come back to the conscious state, although you are in a conscious awareness.

"Although I heard no voice, I was filled with a knowing quality. I just knew things. It wasn't as if the light were speaking to me, but it seemed to give me direct answers to a lot of questions on my mind.

"For a moment I thought that the light was going to form into the Ancient of Ancients. I seemed to have an awareness that it could be a man, it could be a woman, or it could be both. But I knew that whatever it was, it was not anything that I should fear. I think this is what is meant by becoming one with the light and letting your light shine forth.

"If the revelatory experience comes, you become one with it. You must grow into it, become a part of it, let the light become a part of you.

"But learning to grow into the light is a process that cannot be rushed. You must learn to experience the light, let it flow through you, giving it force so that others may feel a portion of it through you. Become a channel for the light, and you will leave a portion of it with whomever you meet. I think that everyone should seek illumination, the process of becoming one with the spiritual principle."

I asked Deon how she would define the spiritual principle.

"I look at it as an energy, a source, something that works within and without and all around us. Something that we can tune ourselves in to by constant meditation, by wanting to help others, by desiring to become one with the universe. By becoming one with the spiritual principle, you, in one sense, give up your life; but you balance your life because you still must live on the earth plane and do the things that other people do. But you must work more and more for others; you must always be ready to help: you must be ready to do whatever is needed of you. You must remember that you are only a channel for God, the spiritual principle; and you must help others become fully aware so that if they should receive this illumination, this spiritual unfoldment, they will know how to handle it correctly."

"Is it possible to subvert this force?"

"Any force that can be used for good can be used for evil. There is a positive and negative aspect to everything. We must keep our own light strong. We must be constantly aware, working in the light, becoming light, because that is why we have been set on the earth path.

"I think that the young people today have come into life with less karma than we older people have. They are more ready to receive spiritual things and to become spiritual. They're not so wrapped up in materialism. I feel that with their knowledge and their expression of truth they're sending out a purer light to the people of today, because so many of them really seem to love each other and to be more truthful with each other than we as a group used to be. Even though their language may seem different, it is a pure language, because to them it is the language of love, and they express it in their voices and in their faces."

One of Deon's favorite theories is that everyone has latent ESP ability. I witnessed an impressive demonstration of this thesis when Deon once noticed my children "testing" one another with the Zener ESP cards.

Deon called to my four-year-old, Julie, who had been playing with her doll while the older children guessed the cards. Once Julie was comfortably seated on a chair opposite her, Deon told the child she would help her guess the cards just as the older children were doing.

"Those symbols don't have much meaning for a four-year-old," I protested, "and I don't believe her attention span . . ."

Deon waved me to silence. "You just look into Deon's eyes, Julie, and call out the card that you see there."

Amazingly, with Deon's psychic assistance little Julie scored thirteen out of a possible twenty-five. Julie's misses seemed to occur when she shouted her guess before she concentrated on Deon's eyes and the ostensible subconsciously transmitted impression.

Seer Daniel Logan, author of *The Reluctant Prophet,* credits the lessons acquired under Deon's tutelage and her repeated words of inspiration and guidance as being responsible for his becoming a career psychic. It was at a séance conducted by Deon that Logan first went into trance. The evening had been devoted to psychometry. Logan was holding some keys in his palm, attempting to psychometrize them, when he began to feel drowsy. His eyes were fixed on a wavering candle flame, and he felt himself drifting away. He was fully conscious of what he was experiencing; yet he seemed to be floating farther and farther away from the séance circle.

Deon told Logan not to be afraid. "Nothing bad or harmful will happen to you," she said soothingly. "I'll be here to guide you out of it. Now, open your senses. Allow the higher forces to take over. Let go, Daniel."

Logan recalls that Deon's words gave him confidence.

"I relaxed and stopped fighting," he writes; "I felt now as though my real self were no longer in my body but that I was floating above the group, looking down on them and on my body below."

Logan heard low mumblings coming from his own throat. Then a querulous old voice shrieked through his mouth: "Bill! Bill! Where are you?"

One man in the circle spoke up and was told in obscene words that he was not the right "Bill."

Deon recognized the voice and manner of her fiancé's deceased mother. She spoke to the entity, telling her she must release her hold on her son.

"I won't let him go, and I don't have to!" the voice shrilled. "You want him for yourself, but I'll be damned if you're going to have him. I'm going to take him, and I'll do it tonight!"

Deon continued to speak in a calm voice. She explained that Bill was happy on the earth plane, that she would lose his love if she continued to act in this manner. Deon told "Mother" she must accept the light. "You'll be alone forever if you don't turn toward the light," Deon added sternly.

Logan says that during the trance his body seemed to shrink, his hands become clawlike. The entity complained through his vocal cords, "The damned pain; my arms and hands hurt, and I can't walk."

Other members of the circle joined Deon in telling the entity that they wished her to turn away from darkness. Eventually a less harsh voice whispered its thanks and promised it would try to release itself from the earth plane and turn toward the light. Gradually the voice became unintelligible, then inaudible, and Logan was aware of Deon carefully guiding him out of the trance state.

Deon explained to the circle and the now-conscious medium that her fiancé's mother had been bedridden with a painful arthritic condition for a year before she died. The once devoutly religious woman had grown bitter. It seemed that the only thing that kept her alive was her intense desire not to leave her son. But at last she had died, a hating, resentful woman. Since his mother's death, Bill had been disturbed by terrible dreams and appearances of the bitter woman.

The day after the séance, Deon spoke to Bill by long-distance telephone and learned that he had had a particularly vivid and horrible nightmare during the time they were conducting the séance.

When Deon's circle met again a week later and Logan slipped once more into trance, Bill's mother returned. But this time the voice was tranquil. After thanking the group for their efforts on its behalf it said, "I am trying to turn toward the light. I will leave Bill alone. I will release him."

Logan later learned that Deon's fiancé was no longer plagued by grim dreams of his dead mother. At that time, when Logan's psychic abilities were still in an early stage of development, he was not completely convinced that he actually had served as a mediumistic channel for the spirit of a deceased personality. But he writes: "I could not argue, however, with the fact that the vocal, mental and even physical characteristics that I had manifested during the trance were (as Deon assured me) incontrovertibly those of Bill's mother."

In a more recent book, *The Anatomy of Prophecy,* Daniel Logan reveals that it was through trance sessions with Deon that he learned the identity of his own spirit guide, Dr. Stanley Podulsky, who, on the earth plane, had been a Polish chemist and pharmacist. Logan explains that he did not mention Dr. Stanley in his previous writings because he wanted to protect him from put-downs and to wait until the times were less critical toward psychic practitioners.

It was Richard Speidel who provided Logan with information concerning Dr. Stanley, then requested that Logan prepare himself for trance work, as this would be his spiritual development in the future. Logan recalls that Richard Speidel told him that Dr. Stanley would work through him.

"He will utilize your body and vocal apparatus to accomplish this. There will be many souls that will be guided by Dr. Stanley. You will learn much from your association with him yourself. You are to be the channel through which Dr. Stanley will work, a vessel for his being."

Deon Frey has often served as a vessel for intelligences who claim to be spirit entities, and she has touched many lives in her role as High Priestess of the Tarot, as Spiritualist minister, and as a teacher in the most arcane tradition of Real Magick. Privileged, indeed, are those few who have received private tutelage in the esoteric arts from this most gifted woman. Deon Frey is certainly one of those individuals who have worked diligently, both in the public's awareness and behind the scenes, to make Chicago North America's most psychic city.

—6

Joseph DeLouise— from Poor Kid to Prophet

JOSEPH DELOUISE HAS found out that the gift of prophecy can get a guy into trouble no matter how well-meaning he may be.

The March 23, 1973, issue of *The Wall Street Journal* took notice of DeLouise's prognostic prowess by stating that although he has never read a stock analyst's report, knows nothing about stock charts, and rarely reads newspaper business pages, some of his predictions had proved "eerily accurate."

"In late 1968," the *Journal* summarized, "he predicted in a newspaper article that the Dow-Jones average would drop below 750 during 1969–70. In another newspaper article, in late 1971, he forecast the market would break 1,000 in September 1972 (it did it in November) and that the price of gold would double from the then-current price of about $40 an ounce (it did so in early 1973)."

Joseph was feeling pretty good about such prestigious recognition. Not bad for a kid from Sicily who emigrated to Chicago with his parents when he was only six. How about that? *The Wall Street Journal* writing about a poor kid who grew up in one of the toughest slum neighborhoods in the city. A kid who never got past the eighth grade, who managed to enlist in the Navy at sixteen, and who, after World War II, made it through hairdressing school so that he could open a beauty parlor.

But then came a warning from the Securities and Exchange Commission (SEC), which governs the nation's stockmarket activities, to stop commenting on "stocks, bonds, the Dow-Jones averages or the price of gold or face prosecution." Edward Harmelin of the Chicago offices of the SEC warned Joseph DeLouise that he could be in violation of the 1940 Investment Advisors Act if he were to continue to discuss the market with his clients.

Joseph was confused and a bit frightened after he received the first call. "They sounded like they really meant business!"

He cleared his head, called his attorneys, and asked the SEC to repeat the warning. They did.

Tom Valentine reported the next steps in the imbroglio in the June 24, 1973, issue of *The National Tattler:*

> DeLouise's lawyers, Sam Elliott Pfeffer and Robert M. Salzman, explained: "If our client . . . pays $150 and applies for a license, he may be given the right to advise others on the stock market.
>
> "However, Joseph is not a financial consultant. In fact, he knows absolutely nothing about the market except what impresses him psychically. He has no scholarly expertise, and it would be fradulent for him to apply for such a license."
>
> Pfeffer explained that DeLouise expresses only his

perceptions and tells his listeners whether he has a good feeling or a bad feeling about the market.

"He has a constitutional right to express his psychic feelings," he said.

The staff of the SEC offices in Chicago disagreed with Joseph's attorneys. As they saw it, the psychic-sensitive could be charged under the 1940 act and fined ten thousand dollars or given two years in jail—*or both.* A spokesman for the SEC advised Joseph that he could not even discuss the stock market when he was being interviewed by news media. Comments about stocks and commodities during lectures were, of course, forbidden.

Joseph tried to explain that he received his impressions mentally and spiritually. The reception of such impressions was a religious thing with him. By no stretch of the definition could Joseph DeLouise pretend to be a bona fide stock market consultant. He was a mystic, a psychic-sensitive.

At last the SEC appeared to relent, for Joseph continued to make economic predictions for newspapers and clients based solely on his psychic attunement, not his financial acumen.

If the SEC had charged DeLouise with violation of the 1940 Investment Advisors Act, it surely would have been a landmark case. Think of the thousands of skeptics and detractors of psychism who would have been in the uncomfortable position of having a security branch of their government prosecuting a psychic-sensitive for being *too accurate* in his advice and for predicting peaks and valleys in the Dow-Jones averages.

But Joseph DeLouise doesn't like trouble. He is a soft-spoken, gentle, considerate man. I remember the concern that hung heavy on his words when he telephoned me to discuss the charges the SEC was attempting to levy against him. Joe was hurt and confused. I was happy that he did not have to go through a difficult courtroom battle, because gentle man that he is, I know that his psychic gifts are so important to his very life that he would have carried the fight to the highest court in the land.

Tom Valentine, a fellow author in the psychic field and Joe's biographer, has expressed his opinion that DeLouise ranks among the top six seers in the world today.

I would not dispute that assessment, for Joseph DeLouise has realized some remarkably accurate predictions in the years since he achieved national prominence with his previewing of the collapse of the Silver Bridge across the Ohio River at Point Pleasant, West Virginia, December 15, 1967. Since that dramatic hit, DeLouise has accurately, and well in advance of the event, predicted train crashes, airline tragedies, political crises, and the aforementioned stock-market fluctuations.

Some of Joseph's more exciting work with police authorities was done in regard to the grisly Sharon Tate murder case in August of 1969. I remember Joe telling me that, about four or five days after the murders, he was contacted by a fellow who used to live in Chicago who knew of his having found buried treasure through psi abilities. The man acted in no official capacity, but he did put DeLouise in touch with Mary Neiswender, a staff writer for the Long Beach *Independent Press Telegram,* who later wrote articles based on his psychic observations.

Reviewing my notes of DeLouise's predictions six years later, I find that Joseph described one of the killers as being tall, about 160 pounds, with darkish blond hair, blue eyes.

DeLouise saw the dominant member of the group as being "Mediterranean-type," with dark hair, short in stature, slight of build.

Charles Manson, the leader of the "family" is five feet seven inches tall, with dark brown hair and brown eyes.

Joseph saw one of the suspects in Texas, felt that another of the suspects might be a mechanic, and received September 14 as an important date in the case.

One of the suspects was apprehended in Texas; the Manson "family" had provided for themselves by stealing Volkswagens and converting them into dune buggies for resale; police authorities first received a clue to the accused cultists on September 15, 1969.

DeLouise said that a girl by the name of Linda would be important in the case. He also felt that black magic and drugs had been involved in some way with the murders.

DeLouise's "Linda" turned out to be Linda Kasabian, the family member who turned state's evidence after her arrest and whose testimony helped to convict Manson. The bizarre family did practice strange rites based on perversion of occult practices, and they were heavily into the unrestrained drug trip.

At the time, Joe told me: "If the truth behind these murders ever really comes out, there will be a terrible black eye for Hollywood. Several big names will come out of this case if it is allowed to progress. A lot of Hollywood has been playing with black magic without knowing the problems that they have been bringing on themselves."

At this writing (June 1975), the rumors still persist. There have been assertions made by many "insiders" to the Hollywood scene, as well as various counter-culture groups, that the seeds planted by Charles Manson have not yet been thoroughly uprooted, that there are many flowers of evil waiting to bloom.

When the Manson case came to trial, one of Manson's girlfriends came to Chicago to beseech Joseph's help in locating Ronald Hughes, the lawyer for the "family" who mysteriously disappeared during the trial. Such a request appealed to Joseph's sense of poetic justice, and he flew to California.

Once on the West Coast, DeLouise found that the negative vibrations of the Manson people caused him great inner confusion; but he was still able to receive a clear mental image of Hughes lying dead in a mountain culvert. When the police followed through on DeLouise's psychic lead, they found the attorney's body only fifty yards from the spot Joe had pinpointed on a map.

Joseph went on from the Manson case to assist the San Francisco Bay Area police with their infamous Zodiac killer, a mysterious sniper who goaded police and the press with announcements in the newspapers prior to his murders. Zodiac has never been captured, and the case remains open. DeLouise feels that although the deadly sniper continued his slayings for two years, there will be no more crimes due to Zodiac's deadly aim. "I get the strong impression that Zodiac is dead," Joseph says.

Here are notes I made of DeLouise's impressions of the Zodiac killer at the time he was working on the case:

"I see a man about twenty-eight years old, about five feet eight inches tall, about 145 pounds. He has done newspaper or police work, and he is familiar with police procedure. He may at one time have worked around horses. He is a lonely man. He loves flowers, but he hates the police. His early murders were committed to bug the cops. I feel that he may have been rejected for a job or a job advancement, and this rejection set him off.

"I keep getting the words 'Roth' or 'Robert,' and I keep hearing 'field,' maybe 'Fairfield.'

"He became the Zodiac to throw people off his track. He doesn't really know much about astrology, but he does know code work and he has served in the Army. Zodiac has led a very messed-up life. I feel his father was an alcoholic. He's an Aquarian; I picked up February.

"He could be an ex-policeman. He could be a policeman's relative. Someone is inadvertently giving him information, because he knows too much about the police and their every move. . . ."

Once, just before he left for San Francisco to provide his psychic impressions for the authorities, I talked with Joseph about psychics and crime detection.

JOSEPH DELOUISE: I don't really know if it matters if I am actually on the scene of the crime or not. It helps to touch objects—psychometry, you know—and gain impressions. But whether I am on the scene or back in my office, I try to visualize. When I close my eyes or stare at a wall, I see words, faces, places, just as if I were watching a movie. I think if you set your mind in action and go back and visualize the crime, the impressions will come.

Once a psychic becomes confident enough not to be frightened of being right or wrong, he will be able to do more and

Curtis and Mary Margaret Fuller, publisher and editor of *Fate* magazine.

Irene Hughes personally answers all correspondence arriving at her office of The Golden Path.

Irene Hughes and her "celebrity wall."

Irene Hughes on psychic safari.

Deon Frey, Chicago's high priestess of the Tarot.

more to raise his accuracy. I give people just what I feel. I don't stretch things one way or another. I just have to give what I get.

In other words, you try not to become too emotionally involved.

DELOUISE: Right. I never listen to other people's impressions of what happened, because that sways me. I have to walk out of a room when people start using logic, because logic doesn't always work. At least it didn't work for them or they wouldn't have called me. Like in the Zodiac case, I think when he is finally caught, he will fit the description I gave them.

Did you give the authorities more than a description of the killer?

DELOUISE: I left additional details and names, names that I picked up psychically. I also picked up some locations, and I viewed some of the evidence they had and picked up impressions of specific places to check. There are a couple people in that area who should have been given lie-detector tests, and another person who should be picked up and questioned, as I feel he will be able to give information of importance.

When I arrived in California I made a public plea for Zodiac to give himself up. I offered monetary assistance, and Melvin Belli, the lawyer, offered legal assistance. I said that I would make certain that Zodiac got his story published. I feel he has a story to tell, and I feel that there has been a lot of injustice done to him. In his own mind, I believe he feels justified for committing the murders.

Joe, do you want to make a particular speciality of working with crime cases?

DELOUISE: If I continue to work with criminal cases, I would like to be called in with no publicity, no attention directed to me. I don't want to become self-conscious because I know people are rating me.

I feel that psychics should be given a chance to work with detectives on certain cases in the capacity of consultants. Then, I feel, the psychics should just leave without ever knowing the results. I maintain that once a psychic becomes concerned with results, he will try too hard to stretch his impressions and he will not come up with specific things.

I feel that it is this obsession with immediate, tangible results that prevents the average person from developing his ESP abilities. He becomes afraid of giving his impressions, because he is afraid of being wrong. ESP cannot be developed with the fear of failure in mind.

We have bloodhounds that can sniff an object and track down the owner without missing. I seriously believe that humans can become "bloodhounds" if they allow certain subtle clues to trigger their powers of ESP—and if they learn to project and visualize.

Do you consider yourself a psychic bloodhound?

DELOUISE: Definitely, more or less. There is only one difference. I can go back in time, whereas a dog can't. You could give a good psychic a crime that was committed two thousand years ago and he could probably go back to it.

What is it within you that can go back?

DELOUISE: I don't know. I start seeing pictures. I can turn them on fast through meditation. I have been working on this for over twenty years. I can see pictures when I am asked questions. I feel that once you have developed confidence and the ability to bring forth the rapid pictures, you have got it! Psychics who have to sit down for hours and meditate, and still get nothing, aren't completely developed. If you are properly attuned, you can call for the pictures almost instantly.

I say that with experimentation and co-operation ESP can be used in crime detection. Maybe we are just at the frontier today.

I want to think that I am a part of proving that ESP can be used to aid the police in fighting crime.

Joseph DeLouise feels that man has been placed on Earth to gain perfection, but that he cannot gain that state until he recognizes that there is a spiritual side to life.

"I feel that it is my mission to dramatize the spiritual side of man by reaching out into time and making predictions. My ability to do this opens up the possibility that there really is no time and space as defined in materialist terms."

DeLouise has been strongly impressed that mankind must face some "radical changes" in the next eight to ten years. He fears wars, domestic tragedies, and economic stresses before mankind can take a leap forward. The years 1983, '84, '85, '86 will be crucial, but if these can be survived, Joseph believes, man can begin a whole new direction of history.

Why does Joseph DeLouise remain in Chicago when his work as psychic consultant takes him all over the nation?

"The vibes are here," he answered firmly. "We're either being bombarded with the right gamma rays or the right vibrations or *something* here. The vibes here are just right for growth in the psychic and religious field. Chicago right now is a city of psychic receivers, and their channels have been opened because of these spiritual vibrations.

"As I travel around the country, I tune in and I get different vibrations. In some areas, I don't seem to be as effective as others. But when I come back to Chicago, everything starts to work better.

"Certain areas seem to drain the psychism out of a person. Chicago replenishes it. And I'm seeing more and more people becoming affected in this way. The Chicago area has the vibrations conducive to psychic development, psychic research, and psychic phenomena—the entire spectrum of psi activity.

"And I'm talking about the man in the street as much as I am the professional psychic. I say that if a person is interested in developing his psychism, his channels would open faster in Chicago than certain other places. I mean, it's like if you transplant a flower from one area to another. In some areas it will grow more; in some areas it will grow less. People are going to grow better and faster psychically in Chicago.

"It has something to do with clouds, the altitude of the city, the water in the lake, which make the chemistry and the vibrations just right. I'm not a scientist; I'm only speaking intuitively. But I know that human beings are made up of all different kinds of chemicals, and I know that our chemical-electrical balance is very important. In one sense, we may be like radio sets which can be finely tuned. Chicago has the right chemistry and proper electrical vibrations to 'fine-tune' its inhabitants like no other city in North America!"

In constant demand for readings and personal appearances at psych-ins, Joseph attempts to live as quietly as possible in a Chicago suburb with his wife, five daughters, and stepson.

"I try to avoid any kind of social situation which might end up with me making predictions or doing readings," Joe remarked. "If I'm at a party and the word goes out who I am, I try to be as polite as possible in answering a few questions, then I make as decent an excuse as I can to get out of there.

"I need time for myself, away from women wanting to know if their husbands are playing around with their secretaries, from businessmen pleading with me to predict their successes, from people with their love problems, their missing objects, their domestic hassles.

"You know, I think that a lot of really fine psychics get drained dry by doing too many readings. Publicity can kill a true psychic. The more newspapers are after you to make predictions, and the more you do, the more you tend to rely on intelligent guesses rather than your intuitive faculties.

"Luckily, Helen, my wife, is into yoga; she's a real expert; and she doesn't really ask me to read for her or to make predictions. The kids regard me just as Daddy, and they don't pay much attention to my abilities—until the girls want me to give them the word on a new boyfriend.

"Whether or not having pronounced psychic abilities has helped me become a better father, let me say that the ability to relax, to meditate, can also teach you to develop great empathy. You develop a feeling for people that has great depth. When I discuss a problem with my kids, I can know exactly how that child feels, because I allow myself to become that fifteen-year-old girl. In that way, my psi abilities enable me to be a better father—and a better human being!"

—7

The Ancient Gods Immigrate to Chicago

AS YOU CAN SEE by quick reference to the Chicago Psychic Directory, which serves as an appendix to this book, the Pagan and Neo-Pagan religions are well represented in Chicago. It seems just a few short years ago that I would be asked on radio and television programs: "Tell us, Brad, do you *really* believe in Witches?"

The moderator always asked that question with a self-satisfied smirk that seemed to be telling his viewers that if I answered in the affirmative, he had wrung from me a statement that would constitute absolute proof that I had lost all touch with reality.

My answer was always pretty much the same: "I don't *believe* in Witches. I accept their existence, just as I accept the existence of Christians, Jews, and Zen Buddhists. Witchcraft is a spiritual way of going. It is simply the pre-Christian folk religion of Europe. Pagan does not mean atheist or primitive idolator, as the word is used by certain of those orthodox religionists who feel that they have the only gate to God. Pagan simply means 'country folk,' again indicating that Witchcraft is a religion of nature, of the country folk."

Then, with an exaggerated roll of the eyes and a mock-fearful look over his shoulder, the host would ask: "Do you mean to tell me that there might be Witches right here in our fair city?"

If there was another guest on the show, he or she would usually seize upon that line as a means of regaining control of the conversation: "Witches? How do you spell that? With a 'w' or a 'b'?"

Sometimes, if I felt like being somewhat forceful—or if the host and guests were making an effort at feigned politeness—I would be able to explain just who and what the Witches are. But all too often I fixed a tolerant smile on my lips and spent the remainder of the program quietly counting my teeth with the tip of my tongue.

In the 1970s, however, with so many Witches having come out of the broom closet, so to speak, there are few media personnel who are so far removed from "what's happening" that they still question either the reality or the validity of Witchcraft in our day. Articulate Witches abound, writing books, preparing articles for periodicals, appearing regularly on radio and television talk shows. Psychic Chicago numbers among its metaphysical occult and psychical practitioners some very lively and intelligent Witches.

One could theorize for hours and hundreds of pages as to just why Witches are painted with such dark and negative brush strokes in the Western world. Traditionally, it was the Witches who, with their knowledge of herbs, helped treat the country folks' ailments.

Matters have not really changed all that much today. According to recent studies, the average Witch is basically a do-gooder, seeking to help his fellow man and to influence his environment in a positive way. The principal difference between Witches and the adherents of the more accepted religions is that Witches seek to influence their natural environment directly through hexes and other rituals. The faithful among the Methodists and the Pentecostals, for example, see themselves as pawns of external forces.

Rev. Terry Taylor, of the House of Occult, 3109 North Central Avenue, told me that the culturally engendered stigma associated with being a Witch can precipitate rather violent actions from the ill-informed.

"We've had our windows at the House of Occult smashed six times in the last six months," he said. "Salt has been dumped in our gas tanks. We've been threatened twice with a gun. Someone set street gangs on us. We wrote to the Justice Department in Washington, D.C., and now we have police protection."

I asked Reverend Taylor why, he thought, the House of Occult had suffered such attacks.

"I think it is largely fear," he answered. "People stand outside our store and pass out tracts saying that Tarot cards are a tool of the devil, not realizing that Tarot cards are a path for all mankind. To too many people, anything occult is obviously devil worship. This is their great fallacy. Witches don't believe in the devil."

I suppose that single fallacy, that Witches are devil worshipers, probably accounts more than anything else for the great traditional enmity against Witchcraft.

REV. TERRY TAYLOR: Perhaps, but we just do not believe that there is a devil. There is an active and a passive section in our minds, but neither is necessarily good or evil, plus or minus. Society has programmed so many people to accept certain concepts of good and evil; and the average person, being lazy mentally, would rather accept another person's definition than to seek for himself.

What are your goals? If you had that great, legendary magic wand, what would you like to see happen in the next few years?

REVEREND TAYLOR: It's not a magic wand I need; I need more people who are aware.

I have many rap sessions in the House of Occult, and I

drop a few hints showing the path that exists. There is a key to the system we call life. But you just can't give that key to people until they are prepared to comprehend it.

I take people through a series of classes, and as they progress they become more aware. All of a sudden, when they get that bit of insight, they know the key is real. They think: this poor world, those crazy people out there. But most people just don't want to spend the time to become aware.

I know that you are sincerely interested in helping to bring people to a higher awareness, Terry. What, then, is your reaction to the various media when they run those big exposés of how occultists are fleecing the public for millions of dollars?

REVEREND TAYLOR: If you want to make large sums of money, you don't want to make the occult your business! The majority of people just do not understand the occult, and as we have already stated, a large number of people want to harass occultists and try to destroy their churches, their stores, their way of life. If you are an occultist, you simply can't worry about how much money you are going to make.

I consider myself a fantastically lucky individual. I've got my income, my hobby, my life—everything I want to do combined in one.

I wish that people would realize that there is not a separate god for each religion. There is but one ultimate being who created Earth, the universe, and the galaxy, and he is a god for all. To understand God, you have to understand everything that exists on this planet.

I do believe that there are enough people out there who have inner knowledge from past lives and who, if they are shown a key in this life—and the first key is the proper pathway—can begin working toward God. They probably will not be able to reach that goal in one lifetime; but the next time through, they will realize the key at an earlier age and be able to work on it longer.

Morda, high priestess of a Chicago coven, has a straight job in the mental-health field. "I would only live in Chicago or London," she told me. "I like the ethnic diversity of Chicago."

Morda, as do so many visionary men and women, foresees a crisis period preceding the time of spiritual transition that so many eager seekers have hailed as the Age of Aquarius.

"Before we get to that new age," she said, "there will have to be a kind of burning off of the dross of the soul. I think such crises as nuclear holocaust or ecological damage are going to have to be lived through in order to purify the public at large.

"A lot of people are going to have to reap a lot of negative karma. I don't say that the ones who survive will necessarily be the spiritually superior, but I think they are going to *become* that way because they will have seen how low humanity can sink. Yes, a lot of karma is going to have to be burned out."

Morda received Gardnerian initiation, and she and her husband, Robert, are high priest and high priestess of the Coven of the Sacred Stones.

"We are extremely eclectic," Morda explained. "We do not claim to be traditional. We use rituals from a number of traditions, including the Gardnerian. We are very strongly a healing group."

In addition to her coven responsibilities, Morda does healing work outside her circle, as well as Tarot-card reading, exorcisms, talisman making, and so forth. Robert practices massage, handwriting analysis, and astrology.

I asked Morda to provide an estimate of the Wiccan population of Chicago.

MORDA: I have an extremely high estimate of about one million. Okay, maybe that's antics with semantics, but let me explain. Craft people like myself probably constitute about two thousand people. But then you take all those people who come by it naturally from their ethnic heritage and you get a million.

Now these people may not say they are Witches. They would not use the word Witchcraft, because it has a negative connotation in Western society. But many of them follow various forms of traditional magic. When you consider ethnic paganism and curing, hexing, healing, then I think that a lot of the immigrant population could be loosely classed as Witches.

I would imagine that you resent very much the negative connotation of the term "Witch."

MORDA: It is something that has been very heavy to me lately. My own personal feeling is that we do not want to say that we are something else, because we want to clean up the reputation of the word Witch. It is regrettable, but societies all over the world have this tremendous fear of the Witch.

You know, everything I do is perfectly acceptable to people if I don't describe myself as a Witch. In working with people in terms of healing, I have to keep coming up with other words to identify what I am doing.

I am of two minds on this problem. I don't believe in giving up the name, but I have a hell of a burden to bear if I use the name to identify me. I would never have encountered the prejudice at work if I had not used the term Witch.

Since you work in the mental-health field, would the term "psychic" have been any more acceptable?

MORDA: Somewhat. At least the reactions to "psychic" are generally not hostile.

I imagine Pagan or Neo-Pagan would be almost as bad.

MORDA: Yes. The public associates "pagan" with primitive animism, blood rites, obscene idols, perverse rituals. Most Witches don't like to say that they are pagan, because that sounds like watered-down Witchcraft for the masses. We Witches are just going to have to do our absolute best to clean up our image and present ourselves positively to the public.

Were you born into the Craft?

MORDA: No, I was a believer, though, without knowing there was such a thing. My parents were nominal Jewish. There are a lot of mediums on my father's side of the family. An aunt of mine was a Christian Science healer. My family has been very open, and that has certainly helped.

When I was in my early twenties, I was given some books on Witchcraft. When I read them, I recognized Witchcraft as my way of going. I began to practice it informally. I then admitted to myself that I was ready for initiation.

About two weeks later, I was approached by a stranger who offered me initiation. Since this came from a total stranger, I realized that it was meant to be.

I went to England, lived for a year, and studied the craft with many people who were traditional.

I believe that I first met you right after you had returned to this country.

MORDA: Yes. And shortly after that I was expected to fill in here as high priestess.

I guess it is just happening the way it is supposed to. I have had a lot of difficulties with my colleagues in the mental-health profession, but when I tell them that my beliefs are acceptable to my family, I seem to appear in a more normal context.

Recently, though, one of the Ph.D. candidates in my office asked me to do a ritual for her, and she got the highest score of anyone in her class. She is very bright, and I won't say her score is my doing; but the important thing is that she asked *me* to do this for her.

Ancient Gods Immigrate to Chicago

—8

Henry Rucker—
Healing with Love
and Laughter

"HEY, MAN, DO YOU realize that as we stand here talking my Psychic Research Foundation is burning to the ground?" Henry Rucker said after we had exchanged greetings at John Miller's Midwest Psychic Fair on April 12, 1975.

I had a fleeting memory of Sunday afternoons spent at the foundation, observing Henry and his group of psychics working with people on healing and demonstrating psi development to crowded classrooms of eager students. I felt anguish for my friend's loss.

"No, Brad," Henry smiled, "don't be down. You know we work with what the Father gives us. If He takes things away now and then, He always gives us back many times over."

Who could resist loving a man like Henry Rucker, a man who accepts what the great cosmic flow sends his way, a man who reacts to human need with warmth and love, a man who adjusts to trials and setbacks with a smile?

One time, after listening to Henry deliver a talk to a standing-room-only audience, after watching him move gracefully about the platform, after observing the charisma of the man, I teased him that sometimes he seemed like a combination of Bill Cosby and Father Divine. Henry takes his mission in life very seriously, but he is able to see the humor in his own humanity, his own struggles to achieve a spiritual balance.

Once, I heard several people give moving testimonials to Henry's remarkable abilities as a psychic healer. Then someone asked Henry if he is able to perform such techniques upon his own person. In that soft-voiced, deceptively deadpan delivery of his, Henry admitted that he could not. There were incredulous gasps of disbelief.

"Look, folks," Henry explained. "I love people and I feel for them, and I want to help. Thank God, some people I can help. The love energy flows through me. God does the healing. It's not old Henry doing the job. But somehow there is still a subjective element involved. I can't heal myself. When I've got a stomach ache, I take Bisodol. When I've got a headache, I take aspirin."

Dr. C. Norman Shealy, a neurosurgeon with extremely impressive credentials [director of the Pain Rehabilitation Center in La Crosse, faculty member of both the University of Wisconsin and the University of Minnesota as Associate Clinical Professor of Neurosurgery, author or co-author of nearly ninety papers for professional journals, co-author of a recent book on unconventional healing] has recently completed an extensive evaluation of Henry's healing ministry, together with those members of the Psychic Research Foundation who serve as healers. During a recent conversation with Dr. Shealy, I asked him specific questions related to Henry Rucker:

DR. C. NORMAN SHEALY: In December of 1972 I walked into Henry's office in Chicago and he started to tell me about myself before I had even sat down. He really did a fantastic reading on me. I spent three hours talking with Henry, and by the time I left I had an agreement with him that he would come to La Crosse to work with me on psychic diagnosis.

Did you see Henry do any healing work in Chicago?

DR. SHEALY: No. But on the basis of his psychic reading of me I decided it would be worth working with him. And on the weekend of January 21, 1973, Henry and eight of his friends from the Psychic Research Foundation came to La Crosse.

Had you preselected patients for healing work?

DR. SHEALY: I didn't want to get into healing at that point. I wanted only to work with matters that could be scientifically studied.

We brought seventeen patients down to my office that weekend. Each patient was brought into the room for only a few minutes. No questions by the psychics were allowed. We had previously taken samples of the patients' handwriting and their birth data, which were made available to the sensitives; but the psychics were afforded no opportunity to ask questions.

After each patient had left the room, I would poll the eight psychic-sensitives. When they would disagree on something, I would say now let's vote on it. What do you all think? When we could get a consensus of six of them agreeing, I would write down the answer.

When we put it all together on personality and emotional problems, they were 98 per cent accurate. This is a fantastic record.

By assessing the emotional state of the patient, do you mean the psychics judged whether the patient was depressed, elated, or nervous?

DR. SHEALY: Oh, the analyses were much deeper than that. The psychics provided elaborate discussions of the patients' family relationships, their marital problems, and so forth. Furthermore, they were 80 per cent accurate on physical diagnoses.

Here again, on the physical, these were specific diagnoses?
DR. SHEALY: The psychics clearly gave the correct causes for the patients. Each one was different. For instance, one was an accident victim, another was an attempted suicide, one was suffering from an infection, et cetera. The psychics got each one of them.

Furthermore, I took the psychics up to the ward to see patients who posed particular problems to therapy. The psychics only walked by the doors, and they were able to say such things as, "That man has a brain tumor and he will die." And he did!
Was death expected in that case?
DR. SHEALY: Yes, we had expected death in his case. But the most baffling case I saw that weekend was a man in whom I had placed one of my dorsal-column stimulators two weeks before. The patient had become critically ill. His white blood count was almost fifty thousand. I thought that the shock of surgery had flared up latent leukemia that we had not known about.

Henry Rucker looked at the man and said, "This man does not have leukemia; he has liver failure."

I thought Henry had really goofed. But I had been out of town the day before the psychics arrived, and Tom Beckman, my assistant, looked at me and said, "You know, he's right. Yesterday, while you were still out of town, we detected a very serious liver problem."

The patient still looked to me as if he was going to die. Henry waved his hands over the man—I don't know if he was healing him or not—and said: "This patient will be going home in ten days."

That was on Saturday. On Monday morning, I walked into the patient's room and he jumped out of bed and said: "Gee, Doc, I feel great." I thought that was very impressive!

By the end of that weekend, I was convinced that psychics do an adequate job of diagnosis when they see patients in the flesh. Over the next couple of months, we decided to set up a research project utilizing clairvoyant diagnoses.

The plan was that I would send the psychics a photograph

of a patient, a sample of his handwriting, a palm print, and his birth data. Then the specialists at Henry's Psychic Research Foundation would assess all these data and record their impressions.

Henry did about 180 patients himself, and his psychics at the foundation did about a hundred. This is how we recorded their clairvoyantly received impressions of the patients:

LOCATING SITE OF PAIN

Two clairvoyants . . . . . .75% accurate
One clairvoyant 70%
Numerologist 60%
Astrologer 35%
Graphologist 25%

LOCATING CAUSE OF PAIN

Two clairvoyants . . . . . .65% accurate
One clairvoyant 60%
All others . . . . .50% to 30%

What kind of fee does Henry receive for this work?

DR. SHEALY: I pay Henry a very modest fee. Of course, I don't charge the patients anything for this. Almost without exception, the patients love Henry. I can think of only two who did not like him, and they were so severely psychologically disturbed that they hated everything. In general, my patients think that Henry is better than I am.

How do you judge the effectiveness of a psychic healer— aside from the situation wherein the patient throws away his crutches and walks?

DR. SHEALY: Henry Rucker's interaction with some of my patients is not always something that I would say could be judged as healing. I look upon it largely as psychological counseling. I consider Henry Rucker to be the greatest psychologist that I have ever met!

How would you rate Henry as a diagnostician?

DR. SHEALY: In his ability to assess emotional or personality problems, he is superb. From a physical point of view, he is reasonably good. On the basis of determining the site and the cause of pain from photographs, birth data, et cetera, the psychics at Henry's Psychical Research Foundation were getting about 75 per cent accuracy, which is very good.

Before Henry became a professional psychic, he used to read palms because it was a way to meet people, to get to know them better. Then Mr. Psychic, Clifford Royse, asked Henry to attend one of his psychic read-ins as a palmist. Henry was delighted—and a bit amazed—to find that people seemed to like his type of readings.

Knowing Reverend Royse gave Henry an opportunity to observe séances and mediumship. Later, he became acquainted with Joe East, who demonstrated automatic writing.

"My life was gaining full meaning for the first time," Henry recalls, "yet it was also becoming so very confusing. I had always had a fear of death, but these people were showing me that life did not end with the grave. I had always thought a lot about God, and now I was beginning to get a different perspective about the Father.

"I used to get these pictures of things in my head, and I was not able to understand what was happening. When nobody was around, I would talk to God and ask Him what He wanted me to do. I knew He wanted me to do something, but I didn't know what it was. At that time, though, He wouldn't answer me. I used to shout at Him, 'I know you hear every word I say! Why won't you talk to me?' "

When Henry's parents used to take him to church as a child, he would squirm about in the pew with tears smarting his eyes. He wanted to be a part of the Church, but he could not accept the dogma of hell and damnation. He could not conceive of a God that would make him frail and weak, then punish him for his ignorance and his lack of strength. When he began get-

Henry Rucker—Love and Laughter

ting "pictures" through his psi faculties, his fundamental religious background set up an internal warfare that raged within Henry's psyche for years.

"'Way back in 1944, when I was in the Army," Henry remembered, "a wrinkled-up little Filipino, who seemed as old as the hills, gave me a reading. I believe he must have been relaying a message from God. At the time, the old guy really frightened me, because the things he told me seemed so ominous. Nevertheless, I was fascinated by what he said. I kept the things he said in mind, and I decided that I would do palmistry the way he did."

In the mid-1970s, Henry returned to the Philippines, and he became fast friends with Dr. Tony Agpaoa, one of the more famous of the controversial psychic surgeons.

"I know that there have been a lot of negative things said about Dr. Tony," Henry remarked. "Tony realized years ago that many bad things will happen to many of us in this field. We are going to be called phony, and we are going to be called black magicians and persecuted."

Henry had always felt that he could heal people, but he had been reluctant to claim to be a channel for such a sharing of the love energy. But then Tony consecrated Henry's hands.

"This is the thing that really brought my life into focus," Henry affirms. "My psychic awareness has been greatly stimulated by my healing work. Tony also gave me a talisman, which I cherish. There is something special about it. It has a lot of magnetic power in it."

It is Henry's objective as director of the Psychic Research Foundation (with its new offices at Room 1820, 203 North Wabash Avenue) to bridge the gaps that currently exist between theology, science, and metaphysics.

"I am a black, but I am a Westerner in this life, and therefore I am an activist. I want to stay involved with life. I want to turn on and turn others on and be a light. I don't want to just *hold* the light, you see; I want to *be* it, become *one* with it.

"My own personal satisfaction is in knowing that I am

doing what I am supposed to be doing. My pleasure is in seeing the things manifest that I have been told about. Prominence and popularity are not nearly as important as seeing myself doing things that I know God would have me do.

"Our concepts of religion or philosophy are but measuring sticks to guide us. No matter where we are born, God provides us with these measuring sticks. If we were born in the Eastern countries, our concept of God would be quite different from that of the people of the West. But all views of God are valid. All these different roads lead to one point. There are only outward differences, and they are only semantic. The differences among religions are only the differences of language and interpretation. All religions are saying the same thing: there is something *outside* and, at the same time, inside of you; and you are an extension of this force."

I have always been intrigued by the way in which Henry and his co-workers at the Psychical Research Foundation employ certain African dialects in some of their healing work.

"The particular dialect we use is not important," Henry explained. "We use these dialects in our healing work, because we can control powers which are not known by ordinary individuals. We use them to change the vibrations in a place. By intoning certain vibrations, I can change people's entire concepts. By chanting, I could change vibrations in this room so that a person wouldn't want to walk through the door. I don't do demonstrations like that just to show off or to prove a point, however."

Henry is not at all into idle demonstrations of psychic prowess to impress the gullible and the easily led. "I just want people who might be influenced by me to be able to see life with a different set of values. I want my fellow man to know that he and God have been one since he has been. I'm only a talented vehicle for the healing work. That belongs entirely to God."

I asked Henry what he thought there was about Chicago that made it North America's most psychic city.

"All my life I've been trying to move to California," Henry

laughed, "yet I find myself magnetized to Chicago. It is as if some unseen force holds me here.

"There is a strong sense of spirituality near the lake front. I have undergone a number of spiritual changes there. I've had lots of profound experiences in Jackson Park, Lincoln Park— all overlooking the lake. As a child, there was something special to me about the lake front.

"In my opinion, Chicago is a Mecca, a center where it is more conducive for spiritual development to take place. Chicago is not the place where show-business people gather; Chicago is not the great metropolitan place where the biggest business deals are contracted; but Chicago seems to be the place where the psychics come. By that I don't mean that psychics and spiritual people don't *come* from all over and don't *live* all over the world, but Chicago just seems to be *the* hub, *the* place where people are geared toward the psycho-spiritual movement.

"I have never seen the advantage of going to India or some far-off place for psychic awareness and development. It has always seemed to me that everything that I could possibly need exists right here in Chicago."

—9

Haunted Chicago

I LEARNED EARLY in my life about the naturalness of ghosts. My family home in Iowa has a sporadic manifestation of footsteps sounding throughout two of the downstairs rooms, preceded or followed by the slamming of a door.

As a teen-ager, I was hoaxed by the sounds time and again. Believing them to be the actual arrival noises of my parents, I came down from my room more than once to find that the house was empty, that I had been speaking to nobody —*at least nobody I could see.*

My mother and my sister were likewise often deceived by the naturalness of the ghostly manifestations. On one Christmas Day, all those gathered for the festive celebration were fooled by the invisible guest, whose measured tread on the kitchen floor, coupled by the sound of a closing door, convinced us that a tardy relative had at last arrived.

When I accompanied Irene Hughes on a one-day psychic safari to a large, sprawling mansion just outside of Chicago, and as I listened to the sounds of a ghost child singing in the abandoned upstairs room, I was again impressed by the naturalness of haunting phenomena.

There were other times with Irene when the phenomena took such bizarre turns that impressions of eeriness, perhaps tinged with downright uneasiness (should I admit dread?), caused me to take greater note of factors other than the naturalness of the manifestation. In other instances, with Deon Frey, with Olof Jonsson, the phenomenon became extremely active, and psychokinetic effects set furniture and other objects in motion.

Richard T. Crowe, an expert on spontaneous phenomena, has said that the odds of seeing a ghost in the city of Chicago are probably greater than anywhere else in the world.

"Apparitions and spirits roam streets and cemeteries and haunt houses," Crowe commented. "We even have a ghost house here in Chicago—a house that appears and disappears in the dark of night. This ghostly dwelling is near Bachelor's Grove cemetery, an abandoned burial ground off 143rd Street, near Midlothian.

"As if the thing were not mystery enough," Crowe went on, "old records show that there never has been a house there. But the ghost house appears on either side of the road, at different places. Witnesses always describe it in the same way: wooden columns, a porch swing, and a dim light glowing within."

Crowe said that no one had ever claimed to have entered the ghostly domicile, but he added grimly: "Perhaps those who do never return to tell about it!"

The desolate old cemetery itself is haunted by a mysterious blue light about the size of a softball. According to percipients, the glowing ball behaves in an intelligent manner, even to the extent of deftly evading pursuers.

A Joliet man named Jack Hermanski chased the ghost light on two occasions, Crowe reported. "He said that the light blinks at ten- to twenty-second intervals. He claimed that the light grew as large as a basketball and changed positions very rapidly."

Denise Travis said that she encountered the light in December 1971. She told Crowe that she had put her hand through the ghost light. She claimed to have felt no heat, nothing at all.

I recall an incident that occurred in the Division Street apartment of Rosemarie "Bud" Stewart when one of the unseen denizens that help make Psychic Chicago Haunted Chicago put in a rather dramatic appearance. Joseph DeLouise and his wife; Mrs. Stewart and her son Jeb; my secretary, Jeanyne; Robert Cummings, the Canadian broadcast journalist; and I were present for the unscheduled performance.

I was seated a bit apart from the group in a large easy chair. Due to the arrangement of the room, I was the only one who was able to see down the long hallway that led to Bud Stewart's dining room and kitchen.

As I sat deeply engrossed in conversation with Joseph, I became gradually aware of footsteps approaching me down the hallway. Although I did take peripheral notice of the sounds, I did not turn around, because I assumed I would see either Jeanyne or Jeb approaching me. I was vaguely aware that neither of them was present in the living room, but I had been so involved in talk that I had not taken notice when Bud had sent Jeanyne and Jeb on an errand outside of the apartment.

The footsteps were quite loud, very natural-sounding. When at last I did turn to acknowledge the presence of whoever was so firmly approaching me, I was quite amazed to see no one at all.

I blurted some small sound of wonderment, and the footsteps turned to make a hasty, noisy retreat.

My sudden exclamation directed the attention of everyone in the room to the sound of the running footsteps of an unseen entity. Bud Stewart ran back to her kitchen in time to observe the door of the refrigerator swing open unassisted.

Although our action seemed a bit superfluous, we went through the motions of checking all the doors and windows to see that no intruder could physically have entered the room. In retrospect, this bit of rational precaution seems a bit silly. I had a clear view down the long hallway, so I should surely have seen any physical person approaching me or running away from me had such a personage indeed existed.

A few moments after we had once again seated ourselves in the front room, the sound of footsteps was once again heard coming down the hallway. As before, I was seated where I could command a long view of the hall. The tread of the invisible thing continued until it reached a large cabinet in the hallway, then it stopped and once more ran back to the kitchen, as if we terrible human creatures might be chasing it.

During this repeat performance, however, we were all able to hear what appeared to be the mumble of several voices in the kitchen. None of us claimed to be able to distinguish any words, only a jumble of soft voices. Bud found that the refrigerator door had popped open as before.

There were no further manifestations that evening, but as we discussed the incident, Bud admitted that she had heard unusual sounds in the apartment before that evening's impressive display. On a number of occasions, she said, she had glimpsed the image of "someone" in the hallway. It seemed to me as though the mediumship of Joseph DeLouise, coupled with the apparent sensitivity of Bud Stewart, had activated the residue of whatever ghostly manifestation is pocketed in that apartment.

During many a late-night talk show with my good friend Ed "Chicago" Schwartz on WIND radio, the listeners who telephone to contribute their own stories during the call-in portion of the program have provided us with dozens of remarkable first-person accounts of their own encounters with Haunted Chicago.

Of course an old pro like Ed has heard more than his share of fantastic accounts from the kook-and-krakpot crowd, who clutch their radios to their bosoms as their late-night friend. Many of these men and women, in a desperate move to banish loneliness, somehow summon the courage to dial the telephone and lay an incredible tale on Ed—two parts remembered "Twilight Zone" episode, three parts old story Grandpa used to tell, one part fleeting memory of an old movie matinee serial, and one part the contribution of their own imaginations. But *ohmigod!* They are actually saying it over the radio and zillions of people are hearing *their* story!

Ed can recognize such frustration-born, self-deluded thrilling wonder stories as quickly as I; but there have been many sincere men and women who have truly provided us with what sound like authentic experiences—with everything from mysterious lights in cemeteries to phantom hitchhikers; from haunted lovers' lanes to ghostly footsteps in the attic; from mysterious moans in the closet to apparitions of loved ones at the moment of their death.

Although one darn thing after another has prevented me from joining Richard Crowe on one of his ghost tours of Chicago, I certainly plan to board a bus with one of his groups sometime in the future. We have corresponded quite a bit since we met personally in April 1974, and not long ago we sat down to discuss Haunted Chicago.

RICHARD T. CROWE: I've been interested in ghostly and spontaneous phenomena in Chicago since my high school days. When I was working on my master's degree in English at De Paul University, I became very friendly with Dr. Houck, head of the geography department.

Dr. Houck was always running some sort of tour or other for the geographical society at the university, and he asked me if haunted places might not lend themselves to a tour. I had never thought of that angle before. I plotted out a route for what was intended to be a one-time tour for Halloween, 1973. There was some press on it locally, and we ended up turning away over two hundred people. I got a list of those who were denied the first tour, offered them tours of their own. From that point, I have just never stopped. I run the tour an average of five times a month except for October, which hits ten or twelve times before Halloween.

You take people to sites at which incidents of paranormal phenomena have been reported.

CROWE: For the most part, I have chosen places where phenomena have reoccurred over the years. We range from cemeteries to churches to street corners. Because of the large size of the groups, we are limited to either public or semipublic places.

What sort of things have happened on tour? Have people seen or experienced any manifestations?

CROWE: A very unusual thing happened on the first tour. Cindy Graham, who works in placement at De Paul, is a bit of a camera bug. She was taking slides, and when her slide of the statue of Our Lady of Perpetual Help at Holy Family Church was developed, mysterious faces appeared behind the statue.

We went back to investigate, and sure enough, there were these mysterious images right in the plaster. The paper over the plaster is peeled, and these "faces" show through. Depending on where you stand and how the lighting is, you can make out a few to many faces.

In 1923, an extremely large book was published to commemorate the history of Holy Family. The church was built as a Jesuit parish in 1857, and the Jesuits are very good at documentation. Because of the detailed information in this book, we know exactly when everything was painted, where the statues come from—the whole history of the church. We know that there were *never* any faces painted on that wall. It was just that chance photograph that brought them out. No one knows how long they may have been there.

Holy Family Church, by the way, was built over running water, the Red Creek, and the site of an old Indian battlefield. During the Chicago Fire, the church was saved, according to the people of the time, by the divine intervention of Our Lady of Perpetual Help.

The statue of the Blessed Mother stands in a niche at the

front of the church and hasn't been moved in well over a hundred years. It weighs about eight hundred pounds, and in addition to the mysterious faces, there is a crack behind it. This fault runs from the ceiling to the floor. The fact that the church is still standing, without any support, on a crack that runs the full length of the church from top to bottom, is also credited to the divine intervention of Our Lady of Perpetual Help.

You've told me that several people have experienced something at the grave of Mary Alice Quinn.

CROWE: Yes, Mary Alice Quinn has been nicknamed "Chicago's Miracle Child." She was buried in Holy Sepulchre Cemetery in 1935. She was a little Irish-American girl, very mystically inclined, who is almost the Chicago version of Saint Theresa, the Little Flower, to whom Mary Alice was very devoted. Before she died, Mary Alice told her parents that she wanted to come back to help people. Many incidents have been related, especially in the late 1930s and during the 1940s, of Mary Alice Quinn appearing to people throughout Chicago's Southside.

She's appeared to people in places other than her gravesite?

CROWE: Oh, yes, she has appeared to people around the world! Her gravesite has become sort of a pilgrimage spot for people. They come to the cemetery and leave candles at her grave. They pray on the gravesite. Many people take away handfuls of soil.

Now the manifestation that is most often reported at the gravesite is the overwhelming scent of roses, even though there are no flowers there. During the tours, people have been overcome.

You mean people have fainted because of the powerful scent and the emotional experience?

CROWE: No one has fainted, but the aroma has become so strong that people have to walk away from the site to catch their breath.

Have you smelled the roses yourself?

CROWE: This is strange, but it usually breaks down to

one third of the tour group. I generally have about forty-five people on a bus, so, invariably, when I take a count of those who have smelled the roses, there are usually in the vicinity of fifteen people who raise their hands.

Is there any one time of the year when the scent is more noticeable than any other?

CROWE: I think it is more noticeable in the winter months. Again, there may be a psychological factor involved here. Because of the cold weather and everyone realizing that there should not be flowers around, people may instantly recognize that there is something unusual happening when they catch the scent of roses.

Are there any other unusual manifestations which have taken place during one of your tours?

CROWE: At Saint Rita's Church—which became very famous on All Souls' Day, 1960, when several witnesses saw phantom monks in the church—many people on the tours have claimed to have heard the organ playing by itself. According to some of the parishioners whom I have contacted, the organ played by itself when the phantom monks were seen.

I can't help noticing that you seem to visit a good number of churches on the tour?

CROWE: That's true. Due to urban renewal, haunted *houses* don't last long! Once they're deserted, they're soon cleared away. I have to concentrate the tours on the more permanent buildings.

What about the famous Phantom Hitchhiker? I've heard that she shows up in Chicago, too.

CROWE: She certainly does. Actually, we have a number of phantom hitchhikers. We have a beautiful Jewish girl who has black hair and dresses in flapper-style clothing of the twenties.

How do you know she's Jewish?

CROWE: Because she disappears in a Jewish cemetery, Jewish Waldheim. She has been seen to walk into a mausoleum and vanish. She's been sighted a number of times.

We also have a young Mexican girl who appears between

Cline and Cudahy avenues, just outside of Gary. This phantom was picked up by a cab driver in 1965, and she dematerialized in his car.

To me, the most fascinating phantom hitchhiker is the one called Resurrection Mary, a beautiful, blond Polish girl. We have very ethnically inclined ghosts in Chicago.

Mary was buried in Resurrection Cemetery—which is where she gets her nickname—on Archer Avenue on the Southside of Chicago. Archer, by the way, has hauntings running the entire length of the avenue. It was built over an old Indian trail. So many things have happened over that old path that I think it must be like a ley line [a prehistoric system of aligning sacred power sites].

During the 1930s and 1940s, Mary was often picked up at dances by various people. She would ask for a ride toward Resurrection Cemetery, down by Archer, saying that she lived down that way.

As people drove her home, she would yell at them to stop the car in front of the cemetery gates. She would get out of the car, run across the road, and dematerialize at the gates.

Have you ever talked to anyone who actually had one of these phantom hitchhikers in his car?

CROWE: Just two days ago I received a first-person account from a fellow who picked up Resurrection Mary at a dance. I'll read you a portion of his report, but first I should mention that Mary often varies her routine by getting into cars and giving the driver a story of how she needs a ride into the city.

You mean she literally jumps into the car? Just opens the door and gets in?

CROWE: Right. She doesn't bother to hitchhike; she just opens the car door and jumps in. When drivers see it's an appealing blond, they usually calm down and swing by Archer, where she says she wants off. Then she runs from the car and disappears at the cemetery gates.

Ressurection Mary was also seen just before Christmas, dancing down the street, down Archer, east of Harlem Avenue.

How did people know that it was Resurrection Mary, and not just a happy blond girl?

CROWE: The two young fellows who saw her were instantly aware that there was something very unusual taking place. They stood and watched this girl dance by them, and they got the strangest sensation. There were other people walking by who didn't even notice the girl. The fellows ran home and told their father what they had seen. They never heard of Resurrection Mary, but their father recognized her by the description they provided. I investigated and found out that a week before this sighting, Mary had been seen dancing around the fence at Resurrection Cemetery.

She must really miss all the dance halls that used to be in those old neighborhoods!

CROWE: Here is the report from this fellow. He doesn't want his name mentioned, I hope you understand. I have at least seven first-person accounts of people who have had Mary open their car doors and jump in, but this is the first first-person account I have of someone who met her at a dance and took her home.

Quoting from the report: ". . . She sat in the front with the driver and myself. When we approached the front gate at Resurrection Cemetery, she asked to stop and get out. It was a few minutes before midnight.

"We said, 'You can't possibly live here.'

"She said, 'I know, but I have to get out.'

"So being a gentleman and she being so beautiful, I didn't want to create a disturbance. I got out, and she got out without saying anything.

"It was dark. She crossed the road, running. As she approached the gate, she disappeared.

"I already had her name and address, so early Monday morning, all three of us came to the number and street in the stockyards area. We climbed the front steps to her home. We rang and knocked on the door. The mother opened the door, and lo and behold, the girl's colored picture was on the piano, looking right at us. The mother said she was dead. We told her our story and left.

"My friends and I did not pursue the matter any more, and we haven't seen her again. All three of us went into the service thereafter and lost contact with each other. This is a true story."

You know, Brad, my particular area of interest in psychical research lies in the area of spontaneous phenomena, and there is so much more here in Chicago than I have found in any other concentrated area.

I think possibly part of the reason for this is due to the ethnic make-up of Chicago. I have mentioned that many of the ghosts that I have come across are ethnically oriented. We do have strong ethnic communities in Chicago, and these ghosts seem to be part of the folk consciousness of these people. It is almost as if they support these ghosts through their own folk consciousness.

In Chicago, we have the Old World traditions and we also have their adaptations to the American way of life. We have the grafted folkways of the past, and we have a brand-new type of developing folklore, both functioning at the same time.

I think you mentioned an important point, that of the ethnic groups keeping alive their psychic folkways at the same time that they are melding them with an emergent tradition; but it seems to me from comments you have made that you could also entertain the notion that Chicago might be some kind of power place, with ley lines leading to it and emanating from it.

CROWE: Yes, I mentioned Archer Avenue, among other places, being built on an old Indian trail. Saint James Church, also on Archer, was built on the site of a French signal fort which dates back to the 1700s. Before that, the site served an Indian settlement.

I wonder if so many of these haunted churches, either consciously or unconsciously, might not have been erected over American Indian medicine-power places?

CROWE: That's possible. Chicago is also near the Conti-

Haunted Chicago

nental Divide, which is the portage which serves as the link between the Great Lakes system and the Mississippi system. It is a natural half-way point between these two geological and geographical areas. We do have a number of these power places or "window areas" in the city, and I want to keep hearing from people who have had various experiences in these areas.

Yes, of course, for you are active as a psychical researcher, as well as a tour guide.

CROWE: The tours are sort of my gift back to the people for all the material I've been given over the years. The tours are also my way of showing the people what is happening all around them. I want to help them awaken to the fact that these "spooky" things that go on are really quite natural, quite normal. People can contact me with their information or ask me for information about the ghost tours by writing to me in care of my post-office box, number 29054, Chicago 60629.

In addition to the shades of those who have somehow impressed their image on the physical environment of Psychic Chicago, the city is haunted by yet another barrage of strange phenomena. UFOs are frequently seen in the area, along with misplaced animals, monsters, strange man-animal creatures, winged weirdies, and other bizarre entities that go bump in the night. Charles Fort, that inimitable collector of "damned phenomena," that literary gourmet of delicious little iconoclastic tidbits that simply do not fit any scientist's specimen book or lexicon, would certainly have loved it in Chicago!

Although we may now range some distance from the city-suburb complex itself, my point of contention is that it is still the power place that is Chicago that is drawing these phenomena into a state of manifestation. The entities may spread out in an area that includes most of the state of Illinois, northwestern and western Indiana, parts of western Michigan, southern Wisconsin, and eastern Iowa, but Chicago appears to be the nucleus, the eye of the psychic spiral.

On May 19, 1963, the Reverend Father R. Dean Johnson and his wife were on the western edge of Waukegan, traveling south on Green Bay Road (Highway 131), parallel to Lake Michigan, when they observed a pulsating UFO. As the object grew nearer, they were able to perceive that the glowing object was not just a single light but was composed of several horizontally placed lights. Then, as the UFO came nearer still, they could see that the lights were not external but were windows, showing the interior of a brightly illuminated craft.

Father Johnson estimated the UFO to have been about two hundred feet above them, approximately eighty feet in diameter, fifteen feet high. The object appeared to be gliding at the casual rate of about forty miles per hour. Several cars were pulling off the highway to get a better look at the UFO.

Father Johnson estimated that he and his wife had the object in view for about twenty minutes. The UFO passed over Green Bay Road, over North Chicago, out over the lake, then zigzagged over Lake Forest or Highland Park.

The priest later learned that the object had been seen by those who had attended the stock-car races at the Waukegan Speedway that evening. And when he courageously published an account of their sighting in his weekly church paper, he discovered that several of his parishioners had also seen the object.

In an account the Episcopal priest wrote for *Fate* magazine (January 1964), Father Johnson listed his observations of the UFO: It was no known craft; it was maneuverable; it had not been towed by any other aircraft; it appeared to be intelligently controlled; its flight seemed purposeful; its flight appeared unhurried and made no effort at concealment.

From innumerable phone-in participants on such radio programs as Ed Schwartz's on WIND, I have received accounts of mysterious lights hovering, then darting about over Chicago. On January 23, 1974, hundreds of reports of such a mystery light were turned in to the Police Department, the Adler Planetarium, and the news media.

Nearly all the percipients described the object as a bar of bright light which lingered about thirty degrees above the horizon. The sightings began about 9:00 P.M. and lasted until about 10:30 P.M. As in so many UFO cases, color descriptions varied from pure white to light blue to reddish brown.

A graduate student in astronomy at Northwestern University's Dearborn Observatory described the light as not one bright bar but as at least three streamers of light, one glowing more brightly than the others.

Here is another from dozens of such reports in my files. On May 10, 1973, hundreds of northwestern suburban residents viewed nine bright, pulsating lights in the night sky. The lights offered a varied program, remaining stationary for several minutes, then zooming off at high rates of speed.

Illinois State Police, together with the National Weather Service, attempted to explain away the sightings by stating that a combination of fog and atmospheric conditions, distorting the lights of landing airplanes at O'Hare International Airport, had created the illusion of UFOs. Few who had observed the remarkable aerial display would accept such an explanation, however.

Sergeant Fred Schmidt, who witnessed the UFOs with four other Schaumburg policemen, was one of those who considered such an explanation woefully inadequate to deal with the reality of what had occurred.

"They looked like round vapor lights," he told newsmen. "They were very large and pulsating. There were nine and they were staggered. Some were stationary. Some moved up and down. At one point they disappeared below tree level, and we thought they might have touched down. Then we saw them rise up again to about one thousand feet. They made absolutely no noise of any kind."

As an added veridical detail, Sergeant Schmidt said that the lights on the patrol car he had parked off Schaumburg Road and I-90 had stopped working while he watched the UFOs. "The whole thirty minutes the lights were there, the emergency lights on the squad car were inoperable. But the minute the lights disappeared, the lights worked again," he said.

Peter Reich, aerospace writer for the now defunct *Chicago Today,* had often chided UFO buffs by stating that if such things did exist, surely, in his more than twenty years of writing about aerospace, he would have encountered one. On July 19, 1972, he finally saw his UFO, moving from north to southeast over Lake Michigan.

"I have no idea how high it was," he wrote, "but it was well above the level of my windows, which are on the 38th floor. Incidentally, the windows face north and provide an unobstructed view of Lake Michigan and the sky.

". . . What caught my attention about the flashing red light was that it was traveling at incredibly high speed . . . airplanes never fly that close to our building—and besides, this mysterious red light did something no aircraft could do. As it flashed from north to southeast, it suddenly stopped, reversed course sharply, and appeared to fly along a downward curve in the opposite direction!"

Reich watched the object blink out and disappear at a point near the horizon. He stated that he had never before seen any object "that behaved so contrary to the laws of physics."

According to the testimony of many farmers in Illinois, those same objects which are behaving "contrary to the laws of physics" in the sky are also misbehaving in their meadows, beanfields, and hayfields. UFO investigators are quite familiar with the strange scorched circles that have been left in farmers' fields in the area, and I have often wondered if such impressions might not be the same as those called "Fairy Rings" in the British Isles and those which were called "Medicine (magic) Circles" by the American Indians.

Interestingly, the American Indian tribes took notice of strange lights in the sky long before the European invasion. It is perhaps of even keener interest to note that just as the inhabitants of the British Isles had their fairy tradition and other Europeans had their own versions of the "wee people," so did the Amerindian people have a rich and varied tradition of an interaction with the "Star People."

An Amerindian tale from the area in question could easily be transposed to the British Isles and the Fairy Faith:

A young hunter named White Hawk was crossing a prairie

when he discovered a peculiar circle upon the ground. The circle appeared to have been formed by a beaten footpath, and the curious hunter decided to conceal himself in the tall grass and learn what had created the mysteriously trodden area.

After White Hawk had lain in wait for a time, he heard the sound of distant music coming from the air. His eyes were drawn to a cloud that was descending from afar. As it drew nearer, the hunter saw that it was not a cloud at all, but a basket device in which sat twelve beautiful maidens, each gracefully striking a drum. Soon the basket had settled itself in the midst of the magical circle. The instant the basket touched the ground, the young maidens leaped out and began to dance.

The young hunter was entranced by the beauty of their form and the grace of their dance. The drumming sound now seemed to be coming from the basket, and each of the young maidens struck a shining ball at each step. In his delight, White Hawk reached out to touch the dancer nearest him. But the moment the maidens saw him, they jumped back into the basket and were instantly withdrawn into the heavens.

The saddened hunter returned to his lodge, bewailing his misfortune. He complained to all who would listen how he had missed his opportunity to have a Star Maiden for his own. At night his slumbers were haunted by the sounds of the celestial music and the sight of the lovely maidens dancing in a whirling circle. He at last resolved to return to the magic circle and wait until the maidens returned.

Secreting himself in the grass, White Hawk covered himself with the hides of opossums and patiently sat back to maintain his vigil. He had not waited long until he once again heard the delightful strains of the same sweet music. The basket was again descending from the stars.

When the Star Maidens were engaged in the movements of their dance, the man began stalking the dancer nearest him. But again they saw him and sprang for the safety of their basket.

The basket had only begun to rise out of his grasp when the hunter heard one, who appeared to be the leader, say,

"Perhaps he has come to show us how the game is played by earthly beings."

But the others shouted, "Quick! Let us ascend!" They all joined in a chant, and the basket was almost instantly out of sight.

White Hawk's third attempt to attain a Star Maiden proved to be successful. This time, he disguised himself as a stump near the magic circle. When he jumped up and seized one of the Star Sisters, the other eleven fled to the rapidly rising basket.

White Hawk gently led the beautiful Star Maiden to his lodge, telling her how fine life was on earth. He treated her with so much kindness that she consented to become his bride.

Winter and summer passed joyously for the happy hunter, and his joy was increased by the addition of a lovely boy child to his lodge circle. But the Star Wife was growing weary with life on the tribal confines. She was a daughter of the stars, and her heart was filled with longing to return to her native land.

While her husband was away on a hunt, she constructed a wicker basket inside the charmed circle, placing within it certain objects from the lodge as gifts for her father, the Star Chief. Then, taking her son in her arms and seating herself within the basket, she raised her voice in song and rose to meet a star basket, which took her to Star Land.

White Hawk was disconsolate with grief and spent many seasons sorrowing for his lost wife and son. At the same time, his son grew lonesome for his earth father. Grandfather Star Chief observed the boy's unhappiness and instructed his daughter to return to earth to invite White Hawk to come to Star Land and live with them. "But tell him that he must bring to me a specimen of each kind of bird and animal that he kills in the chase."

The Star Maiden did as she was told, and the joyful hunter gladly returned with them, bearing a large variety of game to present to the Star Chief. White Hawk's father-in-law was pleased by the gifts, and he prepared a great feast to welcome the Star Maiden saw what joy could be had between ...ces, she and her son agreed to return to earth with ...wk.

The magic circle of this Amerindian legend reminds us of the fairy rings, of which an ancient writer said: "They [the fairies] had fine musick among themselves and danced in a moonshiny night, around, or in a ring, as one may see upon every common in England where mushrooms grow."

The fairies, says another authority, referring to the Scoto-Celtic belief, are "a race of beings, the counterparts of mankind in person, occupations and pleasures, but unsubstantial and unreal, ordinarily invisible . . . noiseless in their motion. They possess magical power, but are mortal in existence, though leading longer lives than mankind. Nevertheless, they are strongly dependent upon man, and seek to reinforce their own race by kidnapping human beings. They are of a nature between spirits and men, but they can intermarry and bear children."

The Amerindians divided their supernatural visitors and companions into two categories, those glowing lights in the sky, the Star People, and those who inhabited field and forest, the *Puckwudjinies.*

Here we have one of those cross-cultural references which prove to be so thought-provoking. *Puckwudjinies* is an Algonquin name that signifies "little vanishing people." *Puck* is a generic of the Algonquin dialect, and its exact similitude to the Puck of the British fairy traditions is remarkable. Puck, or Robin Goodfellow, is the very personification of the woodland elf; he is Shakespeare's merry wanderer in *A Midsummer Night's Dream*—"sweet Puck," who declares what fools we mortals are.

Puck is no doubt derived from the old Gothic *Puke,* a generic name for minor spirits in all the Teutonic and Scandinavian dialects. *Puck* is cognate with the German *Spuk,* a goblin, and the Dutch *Spook,* a ghost. Then there is the Irish *pooka* and the Cornish "pixie." To break down *Puckwudjini* even further and concentrate on its suffix, we find *jini,* the

Arabs' *jinni,* or genie, the magical entity of the remarkable lamp.

The Amerindians' two categories for the phenomenon reminds me of John A. Keel's statement in his recent *Mothman Prophecies:* "The UFO phenomenon . . . can be divided into two main parts. The first and most important part consists of the mysterious aerial lights which appear to have an intelligence of their own. . . . The second part . . . consists of the cover or camouflage for the first part, the 'meandering nocturnal lights' as the air force has labeled them. . . . Explanatory manifestations have accompanied them always, and these manifestations have always been adjusted to the psychology and beliefs of each particular period in time. . . ."

As for "the cover or the camouflage" for the meandering lights in the sky (the "Star People"), the Psychic Chicago area has far more than its share of such bizarre activity.

No one has chronicled the "Unidentified Leaping Animals," the "Winged Weirdies," and the "Swamp Slobs" of the area as completely as has my friend Jerome Clark and his research associate Loren Coleman. In a series of articles for that marvelous "bible" for the paranormal and Fortean researcher *Fate* magazine, Jerry and Loren recount such experiences as the following:

September 19, 1970—Six passengers moving along a highway near Pana, Illinois, watched a small, tannish-gray, pumalike creature suddenly appear as if it had fallen out of the sky.

July 1917—A 300-man posse spent several days searching in the woods near Decatur for a creature which several percipients identified as an African lioness. A man suffered claw scratches when he was knocked down while picking flowers. Four people motoring west on the Springfield road were attacked when a beast leaped a distance of twenty feet and crashed into the car, which was traveling at 20 miles an hour. Policemen brought to the scene by the witnesses found the animal still in the vicinity. Since they were not armed with heavy rifles, they chose not to pursue it.

April 10, 1970—A man driving along a dark road on the

edge of Shawnee National Forest in southern Illinois suffered engine trouble for no explicable reason. When he stepped out to investigate, a large, black catlike creature pounced on him and knocked him to the ground. The lights of an approaching diesel truck frightened the beast away. The dazed man now found that his car started easily, and he drove to Cairo, where he received medical attention.

August 1949—Farmers in the New Lenox and Newton areas complained that a screaming animal had attacked their cattle.

November 1950—A creature that roared like an African lion ate forty-two pigs, twelve chickens, four calves, and four lambs—all on *one* night in Peoria County.

April 1964—Something resembling a lion, "only larger," began prowling the outskirts of Joliet between midnight and 1:00 A.M. The thing killed a large dog, ripped open some rabbits, and scared the bejabbers out of hundreds of nervous citizens.

June 25, 1965—Back to Decatur after a 48-year absence, a "black, big cat-like animal" frightened a lady pulling into her driveway. Three days later, it startled three children on an outing in Lincoln Park and gobbled up their sack lunch.

April 9, 1948—A farm family outside of Caledonia saw a "monster bird . . . bigger than an airplane." A Freeport truck driver said that he, too, had seen the creature on the same day. A former army colonel admitted that he had seen it while he stood talking with the head of Western Military Academy and a farmer near Alton. "It was a bird of tremendous size," he said.

On April 10, several witnesses saw the gigantic bird. "I thought it was a type of plane I had never seen before," one percipient said. "It was circling and banking in a way I had never seen a plane perform. I kept waiting for it to fall."

On April 24, back at Alton, a man described it as an "enormous, incredible thing . . . flying at about five hundred feet and casting a shadow the same size as that of a Piper Cub at the same height." Two policemen said that the thing was "as big as a small airplane."

John A. Keel has ventured that since these creatures and strange events tend to recur in the same areas year after year—even century after century—they must somehow live in "Window" areas (apertures in the space-time continuum or ruptures between various dimensions) which permit them to enter and leave our own continuum or dimensions of being.

Or maybe the damned things dematerialize. Perhaps they can exist in our dimension's vibrational frequency only so long before they deteriorate into spasmodic energy patterns.

One of the most irritating factors about UFOs, cat creatures, winged weirdies, and other unidentified leaping animals (ULAs) is that they leave disembowled livestock, slashed dogs, copious unplaceable footprints, even piles of dung littering the landscape; but no matter how often those posses of three hundred men go in search of the creatures, there are no records of any huntsman ever downing one. There appear to be well-documented instances of ULAs having been shot, but no one has ever discovered a moldering corpse or a pile of bones. The things seem only to appear to wreak havoc, scare the blazes out of as many people as possible, then disappear without a clue to their true origins.

In regard to their "true origins," I have wondered if there might not be pockets of energy (earlier people might have called these concentrations "nature spirits") that can take on the vestiges of low-level intelligence. Perhaps for centuries an awareness of such things has impressed upon those humans who dwelt nearby that here there were "sacred" areas that must not be violated.

Perhaps these pockets of intelligent energy may be directed and semicontrolled by human intelligence, sometimes assuming the shapes of the dark, archetypal monsters that lurk in the collective unconscious. Perhaps, on the other hand, these "nature spirits" might interact with us and gain the ability to direct and semicontrol human intelligence.

It has been my opinion that there is some external intelligence which may indeed have two major divisions—the lights in the sky, the Star People; and Puck and his merry menagerie in field and forest—but which has been steadily interacting with mankind in an effort to learn more about us, in an effort to communicate certain concepts to us, or maybe in an effort to confuse our attempts to grasp the true nature of reality.

At the same time, though, I am convinced that there exists a definite symbiotic relationship between us and this external intelligence. I believe that it needs us as much as we need it. It matters little what guise this intelligence assumes. Whether it has revealed itself as Star People, Fairies, or Spacemen, I believe that is has interacted with mankind on a very subtle level for centuries.

The problem we are faced with at this moment in time and space is trying our best to comprehend just what its Reality Game is all about. And why this external intelligence appears to function more frequently and with greater prowess near such power places as Psychic Chicago.

— 10

Eursula Royse— Building a Foundation for Truth

THE FIRST TIME I met Eursula Royse, she was being pulled along the street by an invisible dog. The leash was taut; everyone could see that. And the way Eursula resisted the tugging, the unseen canine must have been rather powerful.

Eursula carried it off straight-faced; but as she walked away from a small crowd of rather startled onlookers, one elderly lady commented to her companion: "What a pretty lady! It is too bad that she is crazy."

Eursula Royse *is* a pretty lady, but she is far from crazy. She is an extremely able psychic-sensitive, who in the two decades of her professional life has appeared in over thirty-five major cities throughout the United States and Canada lecturing, demonstrating psi abilities, and guesting on radio and television programs. And now, after the recent death (June 7, 1974) of her husband, Clifford, the well-known Mr. Psychic, she is the director of the Foundation for Truth, formerly The Chicago Psychic Center, Inc. Is it not, then, good that such a busy lady with so many heavy responsibilities should also have a sense of humor?

One of the highlights of our 1972 trip to Hawaii for the Aquarian Age Festival was being invited to a birthday party for Clifford and sharing a wonderfully happy evening with the Royse family and their friends from Chicago. The only bit of unhappiness during the night was when Clifford and I were visiting quietly in a corner and he told me that he would live but another two years. He had no regrets. He had prepared for the event as carefully as any mortal man might. He was pleased that Eursula had developed into such an extraordinarily fine clairvoyant and medium, and he knew that she would carry on their work in an extremely able manner.

In April 1974, I was pleased to give a brief talk for the Psychic Center, and I asked to see Clifford, who had been terribly ill.

"I'm sorry, Brad," Eursula told me. "I hope you will understand. Cliff sends you his love, but he would rather not have you come to his room. He wants you to remember him as you knew him in Hawaii, not as he looks today."

I did understand, of course, and because of the presentiment that Clifford had shared with me two years before, I was not surprised when one of his students called to inform me of Clifford's transition from the earth plane. My memory image of Clifford Royse shall always be of the happy friend and father receiving the birthday greetings of his associates and his family on that lovely night in Hawaii.

For so many men and women, Clifford Royse was "Mr. Psychic Chicago." Eursula is ably qualified to build upon the groundwork established by The Chicago Psychic Center and to extend its perimeters. I think she was wise in forming the Foundation for Truth, so that people might know at once that a new plant has begun to grow from the seed implanted by another. The seeds may have come from a plant that grew into fruition and transcended harvesttime, but the new plant may bear somewhat different fruit.

Eursula is a native Virginian who comes from a uniquely psychic family, descended directly from the famous English novelist Charles Dickens. Her father, Arthur Bryant, was a disciple of Edgar Cayce, and he strongly influenced his daughter's psychic development. Eursula majored in psychology and public speaking in college, but since early childhood, she has exhibited her greatest aptitude in the manifestation of psi abilities.

Eursula feels that the role of the spiritual in today's society is of extreme importance, particularly since ". . . we are coming into an era when we must generate much more love to our fellow man!"

Eursula conceives of man as being made up of physical, mental, and spiritual components. "In the last ten years, I have observed the feeding of the physical, the feeding of the mental, but the virtual starvation of the spiritual. Even as a little girl, I knew that the spiritual element in man must be fed properly. Everyone must begin to understand that he must move into the love vibration. It is the love vibration that is going to bring us all together.

"Right now, since my husband's passing, I'm probably trying to reach out more to the multitudes, to groups. Up until now, I felt that I could reach people more on a one-to-one basis. I really feel that perhaps the contribution that I have made is in dealing with people on an individual basis and helping them to realize who they are and where they're really going. Everyone must realize the law of cause and effect, that there is so much more to life than the material existence."

Eursula's personal visions have told her that we are moving into a time of great hardships, a time in which the differences between life and death are going to become extremely important to individuals.

"People are going to want to know what happens when they leave their physical bodies. They will want to know more about life after death.

"I believe that people are going to stop arguing about whether or not ESP is accepted in the laboratories. I believe that we're going to have a more complete realization that there is life after death, that we do continue in an existence, that there is a soul that does exist beyond the physical body. The real spiritual mediums will be able to come to the fore and prove the continuity of life after death."

Eursula sees the interest among youth in yoga, meditation, going into the silence, as an important step in our society's spiritual evolution.

"Young people are finding that these various meditative techniques give them an awareness of the oneness of themselves. They learn that they can reach out to a higher force, call it God, Infinite Intelligence, whatever. I most definitely believe that there is a being that surrounds itself in a purity of white light, or energy, and that can elevate and uplift us."

It is important to Eursula that all psychic-sensitives and mediums begin to concentrate on the spiritual-religious aspects of their work.

"Clifford was the fifth generation of mediums in his family. We came back to Chicago because it was his home town. Clifford decided that he wanted to do more work on a religious, rather than purely psychic, level. He became an excellent teacher in this field. A high percentage of the psychics in Chicago have been through The Chicago Psychic Center at one time or another.

"We worked together eighteen years to build what we felt is a firm foundation, and we taught a lot of men and women how to develop their psychism. If we have produced psychics who are only interested in becoming fortune seekers, struggling to get to the top, then those men and women are going to fall flat on their faces. The people out there are interested in the spiritual qualities which exist behind telepathic readings. The seekers feel that psychic abilities prove that there is more to life than the material. They might be impressed by someone being able to read the serial numbers on a dollar bill while blindfolded on a stage, but what they are *really* interested in is how to evolve spiritual qualities which can lift them to higher levels of being.

"Since Clifford's death, I have renamed The Chicago Psychic Center the Foundation for Truth. Now, I don't believe that there is anyone who has all the truth. I feel that each of us has a piece of truth that we can share with others. As we share our bits of truth, we can become stronger and more as one.

"I would also like to build within the premises a lasting contribution to that aspect of truth to which my husband gave so much of his life. I am referring to trance mediumship. I want to be able to present—not only to investigating scientists, but to the people who knew him and loved him—the opportunity to come in and read what Clifford has written and to listen to what he had to say through the use of what we call 'the invisible beings'—those who have made their transition to another sphere."

— I I

Chicago's Psychic Engineer as Metaphysical Teacher

OLOF JONSSON, A MAN who has been able to utilize extraordinary psychic abilities since early childhood, was known first in his native Sweden as the "psychic engineer." Olof retains that title in this country, because regardless of how internationally famous he has become for his psychic feats, he maintains his occupation as a design engineer as a means of earning his living. Olof has certain spiritual scruples which prevent him from accepting money in direct payment for anything he might offer through his psychism.

Olof became a valued test subject for parapsychologists in Sweden and Denmark; and in 1953, when Dr. Joseph B. Rhine, of Duke University, invited him to come to the United States,

Eursula Royse, co-director of the Chicago Psychic Center with her late husband, Clifford, Chicago's well-known "Mr. Psychic," has recently formed the Foundation for Truth.

Typical of the various groups and foundations in Chicago are the well-stocked libraries and bookstores the centers maintain. Here Sharon De-George, Chicago Psychic Center, checks a title in their bookstore.

Henry E. Rucker, President of the Psychic Research Foundation, is garnering a growing reputation as a healer as well as a clairvoyant.

Joseph DeLouise earned early fame as Chicago's "psychic hairdresser." Now, after many remarkably accurate predictions, he is director of Mind Perfection Institute.

Frank Rudolph Young, Chicago's mysterious "Einstein of the Occult," teaches his Zohar Science by mail only.

Chicago's "Psychic Engineer," Olof Jonsson, solidified an already established international reputation with the moon-to-earth Apollo 15 ESP experiments with astronaut Edgar Mitchell. Here the globe-trotting psychic is seen with Philippines President Marcos.

Jonsson soon established himself as a favorite guinea pig for North America's most prestigious psychical researchers. Olof has been tested for telepathy, clairvoyance, precognition, psychometry, and psychokinesis under laboratory conditions. In the United States, as before in Europe, Olof Jonsson has established his title of "the strong man of psychic phenomena." Olof was performing the "Geller effect" of influencing objects with the reach of mind long before Uri was born.

Few psychics have ever matched Olof's ability to accurately guess the order of shuffled playing-cards decks or the proper sequence of the Zener cards (cross, circle, wavy lines, square, and star). Psychical researchers have sought to challenge Olof's clairvoyance by burying randomly shuffled Zener decks days before his arrival at their laboratory or university. Seldom has he missed more than two or three cards. In the majority of instances, he has gotten the correct order of all twenty-five.

It was his ability to survive the tedium of endless runs of card-guessing tests which singled Olof out for participation in the historic Apollo 14 ESP tests with astronaut Edgar Mitchell. In pre-blast-off tests with a doctor who was acting as Mitchell's agent in evaluating Jonsson for the experiment, Olof guessed the sequence of twenty-three out of twenty-five randomly shuffled cards. Jonsson then correctly named the sequence of twenty-five out of twenty-five cards for the doctor, who later wrote: "I must say, in all my personal experience with ESP, never have I seen such an amazing ability so obviously and factually demonstrated."

The drama of the Moon to Earth ESP experiment is now a part of history. Ed Mitchell has resigned from the space program to establish his own Institute of Noetic Sciences so that he might continue to study paranormal and paraphysical phenomena. Olof Jonsson occasionally takes leave from his work as an engineer to go on treasure hunts sponsored by the *National Enquirer* (which have been successful) or highly secret work sponsored by various international governments (the results of which have not been announced).

As a witness to literally hundreds of tests and experiments with Olof Jonsson and as his friend who has shared the confidence of personal triumphs and crises, I have come to resent those who suggest that the gentle Swede has been so conditioned to card-guessing, dice-rolling, and other laboratory devices that he has become somewhat like the rat in a maze.

"Olof is the greatest in the world in the laboratory," some psychics have admitted, "but I do my best work with people." The unspoken suggestion in such a statement is, of course, that Olof has become a mechanistic psychic robot, so programmed to perform for parapsychologists that he has surrendered a portion of his humanity.

I wish to go on record as stating that such is most emphatically not the case. To know Olof Jonsson well is to know a warm, considerate, almost saintly individual. He is a mystic of great depth of insight and feeling. He has much to share and a great deal to teach. Several men and women approached me after the publication of our book *The Psychic Feats of Olof Jonsson* to tell me how uplifted they felt after reading Olof's concluding words in the volume.

I would like to quote the final paragraphs of that personal credo, then share with readers a discussion with Olof Jonsson the psychic engineer as a metaphysical teacher.

"No man needs to be afraid of dying. The order of Nature, the Cosmic Harmony of the Universe tells us that in all forms of existence, everything has meaning, nothing comes about by chance. It is blasphemous to believe that man alone should be excluded from the orderliness and purposefulness of the Universe. The secret of life's course and death's chambers is found within each of us in the unknown levels of the unconscious, wherein lie many dormant powers.

"The utilization of the powers, the 'sparks of divinity,' within each of us, should never tempt the wise to make a religion out of spiritual blessings that have been dispensed to all men. Rather, an awareness of the powers within should serve to equip the interested and the receptive with a brilliant searchlight on the path to Cosmic Harmony.

"It is in one's own home, in his own little chamber, in moments of quiet meditation that a stream of the great light of Cosmos is best able to reach in and enrich the soul and open the eyes to the magnificent and tranquil gardens that lie beyond the borders of the Unknown. That which governs a man's life is neither chemistry nor physics nor anything material, but the proper spiritual link-up with the powers within his own psyche and the blessed Harmony that governs the Universe."

Is psychism a natural human faculty, possessed by every human being to a greater or lesser degree, or is it acquired by mystical enlightenment?

OLOF JONSSON: I believe that psychism is a natural human faculty possessed by every human being. There are cases of people who have had mystical experiences or revelatory experiences which have changed their lives, and they have had a sudden dramatic development of psychic ability. But this is very rare.

Is it possible to teach the abilities you possess as a psychic-sensitive, or must each individual seek his or her own enlightenment and path to psychism?

JONSSON: Although I was born with these abilities, I do believe it is possible to teach, or to bring out, the abilities that each one has within himself. To some extent, I am able to teach the things that are required to achieve that state of mind necessary for receiving psychic impressions. The student must learn to eliminate all distractions from his mind.

Both Eastern and Western mystics and psychics are submitting to scientific examination to validate their psychism or paranormal abilities.

Will the scientific documentation of exceptional physical and mental abilities, such as you have consistently displayed, revolutionize our understanding of our human nature and that of our universe?

JONSSON: I think it is important to submit to scientific examination so that all may be recorded, even if we do not have adequate equipment to test all these abilities at this time. In all probability, there will be a better means of understanding

Psychic Engineer as Metaphysical Teacher

and testing in the future, but it is important to record everything now so that we may be prepared with documentation for those who follow us.

We now know there are many people with these abilities. These abilities can be developed even if we cannot explain the abilities or the process scientifically. Psychic abilities may help us solve some of the problems we have today in various fields, such as medicine, the arts, our creativity. They may help us to live in harmony with our fellow man.

Do you believe there is unity in all matter and beings?

JONSSON: Yes, I believe that all things are a part of the great Universal Mind. All things, all men, all plants, animals, minerals. And I think people who are aware of this live in harmony with nature. This, I think, explains why some people have no fear of animals. They walk through jungles without being harmed. This accounts for people growing enormous-sized plants and vegetation, especially in areas where such things are not supposed to be able to grow. Some people realize reverence for the creative force in all things and benefit from it.

Is there a real hope that new and more improved attitudes towards mysticism and spiritual understanding of a universal nature are possible in the West under the present religious and educational institutions?

JONSSON: I do think there will be new hope toward mysticism and spiritual understanding. I do think, though, that it will not come from any one source or one group. The established religions are changing somewhat now. They are becoming more liberal in their views. We will still have to come a long way, but I do think that science will be responsible for changing the attitudes of the people in the mainstream first. Then I believe the religions will follow.

Did you have a "guru" or "master" who led you into your psychic heritage?

JONSSON: I do not have a guide, guru, or master. I feel the Universal Mind is my guide—through meditation. The information I get is from the Universal Source, much the same as "the river" Edgar Cayce talked about.

Do you believe there is intelligent life outside our planet earth?

JONSSON: I feel at times I have received impressions from intelligent life outside of our planet. I have the impression there are far-advanced civilizations beyond our galaxies. I feel that they have been close to us many times. I do know there are some people who are in communication with these "people."

What is your concept of God?

JONSSON: I do not think God is form as we understand it. God is beyond form. God is energy, but not as we understand it. I don't think we will ever understand the true nature of God until we become one with this Universal Energy.

Since we are a part of God, this part of us that is God-within sometimes will act, pushing aside our conscious mind. Many things happen to people which put them in contact with their Creator. Sometimes it is through an illness, an accident, or some other drastic means—which brings them into contact with God. Other times, it is through conscious contact, as sought through prayer and meditation.

Please explain the force, influence, or power referred to as love.

JONSSON: I do not believe in love as a human type of thing. True love is beyond human emotion. It is an emotion that is reserved for God. It is beyond our personal attachments. Although we refer to our feelings for such attachments as love (and it seems to us as love), I do not think we are truly capable of understanding divine love until we have achieved a high, high state of evolution.

What is evil?

JONSSON: I do not recognize evil as most people think of evil. I will only say that I feel that evil is disharmony. It is the opposite of the warmth and feeling of affection that we hold toward our loved ones.

What is our primary purpose as human beings in physical life?

JONSSON: Although everything has a purpose, I do not

feel we can have any one purpose as a human being. I feel our primary purpose is not in the physical life, but beyond human life. We will not truly understand it until after we have left the physical life.

Do we retain our human personality upon physical death? Are we transformed into "cosmic energy" without human personality?

JONSSON: I do feel we retain our human personality upon physical death. We are transformed into energy, but at the same time we keep intact our memories of our earthly experience.

Have you ever had a formal religious affiliation?

JONSSON: I was born into the Lutheran Church in my native Sweden. I am not now an active member in any organized religion. I do not believe in organized religion. I feel that each person should be his own priest. I feel that it is up to the individual to be attuned to his Creator. I do not say that a person cannot benefit from church affiliation, but, for myself, I do not feel this is necessary.

Can an individual know for certain that the information he receives through meditation is correct and right?

JONSSON: When one receives information through meditation, there is also the feeling that it is right. His life should be guided by meditation and also by information received by the five senses. Meditation alone is not enough. We are given many talents, and meditation is only one of the ways. If coupled with an academic learning, meditation should help the individual choose a path which he considers right for himself.

What is your concept of the human mind?

JONSSON: I believe the human mind is something apart from the physical body. I feel that the human mind is a channel where information is received from an exterior source. I do not feel the human mind is located in the brain, just as I do not feel other bodies, such as the astral body, are located in the physical part of us. Any more than one can put the soul in a test tube, I do not feel the mind can be put in a test tube. We are something beyond the physical body and the human brain. We are mind because God is mind.

Is the human species evolved through genetic improvements?

JONSSON: Although I feel we are evolving through genetic improvements and have made great strides in medicine, we also have to balance this with a type of spiritual evolution. We are also being awakened to things that have nothing to do with the physical. Both are important. I also think good health, good eating habits, and right attitudes of mind are necessary if we are to achieve more human intelligence.

Is there an increasing interaction between the Creator and human beings which is accelerating the awareness of, and adherence to, the spiritual principles taught by Jesus and other "masters"?

JONSSON: Every day, people are beginning to tell each other of their personal spiritual experiences. Before, they wouldn't talk about them. This seems to indicate there is more of a communication between the Creator and human beings. I think we are living at a time when the spiritual principles taught by Jesus and others will be something which is taught to everyone *personally* through his or her own awareness.

Do you see a future species of human beings who will possess superior psychic, mental, and spiritual abilities?

JONSSON: I think that in a time to come man will enjoy a period of peace and spiritual enlightenment. Man will be superior mentally, spiritually, and psychically. He will also be superior physically. He will be guided to eat what is good for him. He will not have problems with obesity. He will develop his will to work in harmony with his Father's will.

Do you see a "superhuman" engaged in other than peaceful activities?

JONSSON: I do not think a human would be "super" if he engaged in other than peaceful activities. I think such a race would not survive for any length of time, although I think it is possible for it to happen, just as the legend of Atlantis said it did. We understand there once were such types of "supermen" but they ended by destroying themselves and their civilization. *Do you see an event occurring that will elevate man to a higher spiritual and mental stage of development?*

JONSSON: I feel we will see in our time a terrible war that will probably destroy a great portion of the population of the world. After this will be a period of peace where man will develop to a higher spiritual and mental state. But it will take something terrible to awaken man first.

Olof, it seems to me that you envision a purposeful universe, a divine plan.

JONSSON: Yes, a divine plan that in the end will be harmonious.

Harmony seems to be your favorite concept.

JONSSON: Yes, harmony is God. When you are in harmony with the cosmos, you feel completely satisfied.

Are there beings, entities, masters on other planes of existence that may guide us in achieving cosmic harmony?

JONSSON: There are forces in the universe, minds that can help us gain information about the true meaning of life. I believe that there is a dynamic force and that intelligences are associated with it.

Who are these intelligences?

JONSSON: They could be entities from other places in the universe. Perhaps they are the souls of those who have died on highly evolved planets, who have left their radiation in the universe, and their intelligence remains as a force for good and for spiritual evolution.

You may interpret these intelligences in any way that is most compatible with your own psyche—as an Indian, as a wise old man, as a holy figure—but they are bodiless forms of benign intelligence. These intelligences may cloak themselves as Tibetans and astral teachers because the human brain will more readily accept an entity that looks like a human being, rather than a shapeless, shimmering intelligence.

You do believe firmly, then, that there are beings some-

*where in the cosmos who are interested in guiding us and help-
ing us achieve harmony and unity?*

JONSSON: Yes, and I believe these beings have the ability
to absorb our actions and our thoughts so that they may know
better how to direct us toward cosmic harmony. These beings
avoid language and work with us on an unconscious level. The
phenomenon of telepathy affords us proof that language means
nothing to the unconscious. We do not think in words, but in
ideas and feelings. What language does God speak? The feelings and the harmony communicated between the unconscious
levels of self comprise the one "language" that all men understand. That is God's language.

*What, in your opinion, is the most important benefit that
one can derive from a heightened psychic sensitivity?*

JONSSON: A great calm and peace that suffuses one's
soul and makes him harmonious with the universe. This sense
of harmony places the minor distractions of our earthly life in
their proper perspective and enables one to be serene and
tranquil wherever he may be.

—12

Zohar Science and Frank Rudolph Young

ALTHOUGH I HAVE NEVER met Frank Rudolph Young in person, I don't know anyone else who has either! Young is the only individual profiled in this book whom I have not known personally over a good many years. But this mysterious Chicago recluse, who is known in certain esoteric circles as the "Einstein of the Occult," intrigues me so that I have been compelled to interview him as best I could for inclusion in this book. The "conversation" I have simulated for purposes of *Psychic City: Chicago* took place through voluminous correspondence from April 1974 to January 1975. I feel confident that my readers will share my interest in this unusual mystery man once they have completed this chapter.

No one will need to speculate, as they do about Carlos Castaneda's Don Juan, if this particular guru really exists, however. Even though you may never see or hear Frank Rudolph Young, you can read his books.

In fact, it was a review of one of his books that led me on a pursuit of the elusive man. In the October 1967 issue of *Fate* magazine, I came upon Tom C. Lyle's critique of Young's *Cyclomancy: The Secret of Psychic Power Control*. Lyle, a steady and accomplished reviewer for *Fate,* termed "Cyclomancy" a new approach to development of psychic powers. Quoting briefly from the review:

> Young applies his own medical nomenclature to physiological functions and regions (primarily glands) about which medical science possesses little or no knowledge. These names include his "primitive Autoconscious" and "Psychic Power Center" of the brain and involve the functions of the pineal, thalamus and hypothalamus.
> . . . Exercises are described to help you develop power to control your body temperature, to "see" with your feet, to see great distances with your "Astral Telescope," to practice psychometry with any object, to see what the future holds for you or for another person, to travel with your astral body, to see through a solid wall, to destroy instantly a bad habit, to influence others with infrared rays from your eyes, to heal others at a glance, to cause your body to "light up" like a human lamp, and to subdue an assailant by psychic force.
> . . . this book shows that the author has done considerable groundwork to bridge the present gap between known physical human powers and the legendary and speculative psychic powers of ancient and Eastern lore. . . . This is a work of experimental and theoretical philosophy, projecting from a thorough background of scientifically sound principles into the as yet unknown psychic field. . . . When demonstration of psychic powers achieves recognition as a laboratory science, this might well prove to be the manual on fundamentals that made such progress possible.

Strangely enough, for a book of "experimental and theoretical philosophy" which might one day be *the* manual that helped psychic phenomena achieve recognition as a laboratory science, *Cyclomancy* is out of print. According to Young's publisher, Parker Publishing, he has written eight books for them, but three, including the one that bridges "the present gap between known physical human powers and the legendary and speculative psychic powers of ancient and Eastern lore," are no longer available in this country.

The biography provided on the jackets of his books make Frank Young sound like an ideal hero for a series of Doc Savage-type adventure novels. He claims to have descended from a line of yogis that dates back nearly one hundred fifty years, and from a chain of doctors and dentists nearly two hundred years long. Certain of his ancestors had been in close touch with the *cimarrones,* a secretive tribe made up of slaves who escaped the Spanish conquistadors to establish their own under-jungle cities in the wilds of Darien (Panama). The *cimarrones* were well known for their psychic miracles, and Frank inherited a treasury of never-before-revealed secrets from them.

I found out that Young never lectured, never made public appearances, and never granted interviews. Almost by accident, however, I contacted a source that published his shorter courses before they were expanded into books, and they arranged a "by mail" meeting for me. Although Frank Rudolph Young guards his privacy with a fervor I have never before encountered, he proved to be a most frank and courteous correspondent.

I am certain that the following interview will provoke reader response, so at the outset permit me to request that no one swamp me with inquiries for additional information about the man. His books are available at bookstores everywhere, and polite letters that include a stamped, self-addressed return envelope may receive a personal reply if directed to his attention in care of Clarion, Box 2109-R, Chicago, 60690.

Why do you so oppose speech as a means of communication?

FRANK RUDOLPH YOUNG: The moment I meet anybody, I feel his thoughts shoot through my whole nervous system. Even if I don't read his thoughts—for I don't claim to be a mind reader—I feel intensely his reactions toward me, no matter how subtle they are. I also feel, as I associate with him, the "approvals" or "disapprovals" of his thinking, even when he is silent.

Everybody has this ability. Mine, though, is so much more explosive than most other people's that when I am in anybody's company, it repeatedly tightens or relaxes my whole body. When I converse, I feel it keenly in my vocal muscles, and it can make my speech too hasty or throw it into a stutter or shut it off completely or into a stammer.

The more physically fit I am, the more keenly I react in this manner, because my nerve electricity is then popping with its highest millivoltage like a sprinter ready for the starting gun.

The few times in life when I drank to intoxication, while in college, I lost that super-keenness and relaxed all over without effort. But I also lost my psychic power. The other person became like a lamppost to me. I was no longer supersensitive to his thinking until he spoke and revealed his thoughts to me. Since people don't always tell you their exact thoughts, I extracted from my companion then only what *he* wanted me to know. To possess psychic power—psychic supersensitivity— you have to oversensitize yourself into the super-stutter state, like that of the medium in action.

Most, and perhaps all, mediums in the trance turn incoherent or speechless! Winston Churchill, Bernard Shaw, Moses, Aristotle, and other super-psychics and geniuses stuttered and stammered, except when they took extreme measures to restrain themselves day by day. A stutter-stammerer, I believe, is an individual who has progressed beyond the stage of speaking almost into the non-speaking, ESP stage of life! Everybody will eventually reach that stage in his physical and spiritual evolution. The stutter-stammerer is already one plane ahead of him and will reach it first.

To transform yourself into your super-self, which I teach in my shorter courses and full-length books, you have to supersensitize yourself to the other person, or throw yourself physiologically and aurally into the super-stutter state. But instead of speaking to him in that state and making a fool of yourself, you promptly *de*-sensitize yourself to him again and relax your whole body, so that you can use what you just extracted from him psychically to your utmost advantage. If you didn't have to communicate with him with the handicap of oral language, but could do so exclusively with psychic power, you could *remain* in your super-psychic stutter state and communicate with him with the speed and thoroughness of a computer.

That's why, I repeat, speech is a nuisance. It is communication pollution! A glib, facile tongue merely indicates that the speaker has either memorized beforehand what he is saying, or is practically *non*-psychic at the time and is missing out on the concealed reactions of the other person to him.

And you aren't at all interested in appearing on radio or television to discuss your work?

YOUNG: *Cyclomancy* broke the occult ice in this country —or in the world. Previous to it, all you heard scientifically about the occult was an occasional mention of the experiments of Dr. Rhine and a few other laboratory men. Once my book was published, however, the occult explosion started.

I could have rushed to New York then and capitalized on it without limit. The book sold about fifteen thousand copies in the first mailing. Advertisers copied it right and left. All of a sudden, everybody was offering courses and gadgets to "see through walls," "peer 200 miles away with the naked eye," "overhear conversations 10 miles away," and so forth.

Cyclomancy did demonstrate how the psychic masters achieved those powers and taught the reader how to do likewise. But it insisted that the average man should be satisfied to acquire but one hundredth or less of such powers, and that he would be so unusual that he would become a superman in practically anything he wanted to.

Why is such an unusual book out of print after four printings?

YOUNG: Simply because too many new readers found it too profound, too far in advance of their times. I had refused to simplify it before my publication, as my publisher had implored, because I didn't want every Tom, Dick, and Harry to procure it just to try to get rich in a hurry or to bring others under their control and subject them to the enslaving powers of the "Psychic Harpoon" and others which I thoroughly described and showed how to master.

I preferred to keep this previously carefully guarded knowledge so deeply scientific that only the sincere student would concentrate on it and extract these far-ahead-of-the-times secrets, just as the alchemists concealed their fabulous secrets for centuries. *That* person—that *deserving* person—could make a superman of himself (or herself) and truly attain wealth, health, body power, X-ray vision, and all the powers described, in exceptionally fast time. So, I had limited the numbers who would master it, and thereby favored those who were sincere.

I refuse to promote my books to the masses with lectures, radio, or TV appearances. I prefer to let the deserving readers come upon them however they may. Foreign countries seem to find them. Americans can do likewise—or just do without them.

I have been begged for years, too, by readers and students of my books and courses to open institutes across the country. I have resisted doing so for twenty-two years. Some students have been after me to do this for as long as fifteen years, and they feel disappointed and resentful because I have not done it.

But it takes time and investment to set up schools, and the kind of books I write leave me little time. And since I don't promote them as other authors do, they don't bring me very much money. I would also have to train qualified instructors and have office space for clerks to keep records and handle the transactions. To turn into a business executive myself would rob me of time for making more psychic discoveries far ahead of those behind the Iron Curtain and for conducting the research and secret experiments necessary for my books. As soon as such a setup is arranged, though, I will start letting my faithful followers know. As they themselves master my teachings, I will license them to open classes and teach them to others, in suitable locations.

I will show you about twenty-four or twenty-five of the historic psychic discoveries I have made, but my two books *ıancy* and *Psychastra* contain about three or four ..uııured of them all together. The behind-the-Iron-Curtain scientists have only discovered, in their titanically subsidized way, about fifty-four of them. And they have explained them *in practically the same words and with the same principles of physics or physiology* that I used. In the next thirty-five years, I expect them to discover and explain close to another two hundred of my findings. In the meantime, though, I am making still more incredible psychic discoveries.

The power to radiate thoughts. I discovered and taught this ability scientifically twelve years before the Russians.

Weather influence. Soviet scientists announced in 1968 or 1969 that psychokinesis (PK) diminished in stormy weather. I taught and published the same three years before them.

The power of the mind over a "force field." Four years before them.

Molecular action in "force field" to control the movements of objects with the mind. Four years before them.

Invisible hypnosis. Nine years before them.

How to rule others with your thoughts. Fourteen years before them.

Telepathic rapport. Soviet scientists publicly confessed in 1968 their suspicion that a psychic enters into rapport with another person's brain whenever he wants to affect him in any way. I taught and published how to do this with "chain rapport" fourteen years before them.

Beaming negative ions at would-be psychics to "facilitate" telepathy. Fifteen years before them.

The secret of achieving boundless rapport with animals— even with the most fierce. Sixteen years before them.

How to alter yourself with psychic power into an entirely different and much greater person. Twelve years before them.

Gamma brain waves for deep psychic power. Two years before them.

Trying to open up the secret powers of the mind and train them—with hypnosis. Sixteen years before them.

Objects leaving color traces in the air after being removed. The Russians call it "eyeless sight." Thirty-one years before them I taught this closely guarded Zohar Science secret to a desperate gold prospector in Central America. With its help, the prospector found a fantastic gold cache.

The miracle of the different polarities between the front and back of the living body—and how to use it for superhuman purposes. Two years before them.

The etheric body—the invisible body—the only channel through which mind and life may communicate with the physical shape. In 1967 and 1968 the Russians discovered the closest thing to the "invisible body" and called it the "biological plasma body." They described it as being composed of ionized, excited electrons, protons, and possible other particles, and that it gave off its own electromagnetic fields.

One year before them, I taught and published that it was a gas or a *plasma.* I described its probable physical and chemical composition as including *electromagnetic radiations* and that it was affected keenly by different brain waves and by the *alkalinity and acidity* of blood. (The alkalinity and acidity of blood is created by *ionized, excited electrons* and other factors. Practically the very words and explanations the Russians used!)

The human lamp. Ten years before them, I already taught and published how to create it.

Sudden, strong emotions (besides pain) bring changes of color and of light emanating from the body. Four and five years before them.

Changing the life force (the vital energy) deep inside the body. For thousands of years the Chinese did it with acupuncture. I describe this life force, or vital energy as "The Dynamite Concealed in Your Protoplasmic Irritability," and I have taught and published how to do it *without* acupuncture, since 1966.

To change the actual molecular structure of water with psychic power. I taught and published how to do so thirteen years before the Czechoslovakians showed such a secret film to the authors of *Psychic Discoveries Behind the Iron Curtain.*

Multiplying psychic power energy. The Czechs did it with a created "telepathic generator." Four years before, I taught and published *How to Increase the Drive of Your Psychic Power Command* without storing it in a "machine."

"Staggering or assaulting" others from a distance with psychic power. The Czechs found that they could do it with the "telepathic generator." Three years before them (after teaching it for a long time before that), I published how to do it with the "Psychic Harpoon" (for worthy purposes only) with *psychic power alone.*

The front part of the brain is many, many times more powerful for psychic power than the back part. I discovered this several years before the Russians.

Telepathy can be transmitted to a person who is not even aware that the transmission is taking place. Eight years before a leading American parapsychologist showed psysiological proof of it.

The possibility of transferring energy from living bodies to nonliving matter. I showed how, four years before the Bulgarians did it.

Is bio-plasmic energy necessary for ESP? The Russians say "yes." But I declare that "No plasma flow is necessary for bio-plasmic energy. *Protoplasmic irritability is the true medium* which induces your aura to move around through your tissues."

What is the difference between cause and effect? A leading Russian scientist considers the energy known as "the rate of flow of time" as being the difference between cause and effect.

I disagree with him and call that energy "Action-Reaction." Time is merely the medium through which cause and effect take place. I define Action-Reaction as a thought and response, a visualization-perception. This is *tremendously important* for creating shattering psychic power!

Through the nearly century-long association of my ancestors and myself with the Voodoo Cimarrones in the Andean jungles, I will reveal the fantastic myo-feedback: the muscle-mind feedback. With my extensive knowledge of medicine, dentistry, and chiropractic, I have perfected their techniques and taught them to selected numbers of people. The results have bordered on the miraculous. Myo-feedback outdates the brainwaves and the machines!

What type of educational background do you have? Heavily scientific?

YOUNG: I am the proud kick-out of two leading universities! My big failure was my *not* being kicked out of the third! I degraded my talents so much in that one, in fact, that I graduated with an A— average and earned a doctor's degree besides! I'll never live that one down! Colleges are little more than camera-mind institutions.

In Northwestern University Dental School, I was flunked in the first semester of anatomy. The semester's work was limited to the head, but I spent most of the time investigating the pineal gland on my own and insisting, to the professor, that it contained psychic powers which have, thirty years later, been attributed to it. (I passed the course easily the second time by keeping my mouth shut.) In the physiology laboratory, too, in my sophomore year, instead of concentrating on vivisecting the dogs, I secretly conducted psychic-power experiments with brain waves.

So enmeshed was I in my secret psychic investigations already that I hardly did my work for the different classes. At the end of the term I showed up for only one examination, immediately handed in a blank paper with my name, and bewildered the examiner by shoving it under his nose and walking out. So they gave me the boot, with the postscript that I would never be accepted back. That was my proudest day. I had stopped being an academic zombie!

What made you think of brain waves, which were just being discovered then, as being linked up with psychic power?

YOUNG: Aside from my ancestral background, I had been researching the occult from a mere boy, right in the midst of the Voodoo center in the Republic of Panama, where I had been born of a Scotch-Irish mother and of an English-Spanish-East Indian father."

What did you do after being kicked out of the universities?

YOUNG: I was penniless, so I went into physique modeling for sculptors and did part-time bus-boying, to keep myself alive while I proceeded singlehanded with my occult investigations.

A scout for Universal Studios discovered me, and I was

urged to go at once to Hollywood. I was cast immediately into the leading role of a bullfighter, with elaborate plans to make me the big romantic star of the day, the successor to Rudolph Valentino. But to my impatient mind, the picture took too long to get started, and I was dying to sink my teeth back into occult research. So I walked out of Hollywood, lived in Los Angeles on odd, ill-paying jobs whenever I could find them, and spent the remaining hours rounding out my knowledge in the public library.

I was now using my own mind, my *creative* mind, my *individual* mind in full swing. My hidden powers swung into full use! I determined to read and master at least one book from each department of the library. I didn't read to memorize to pass examinations, but for *my own* curiosity, for my own tracking down of whatever puzzled me.

How did you proceed with your occult research?

YOUNG: I met Cheiro and other leading psychics and learned secrets which they have never put in print. But my leanings were too scientific for them to follow, since my education had been strictly along medico-dental lines. Not only that, but my interest in history and politics remained insatiable after New York University.

Frank, you have sent me a most impressive list of predictions which you made well in advance of the actual occurrences. How can one be positive that he is making an accurate prediction when it is so easy to be misled by one thing or another?

YOUNG: By watching five important obstacles which constantly threaten to ruin the very best predictions:

1. WISH THINKING. A desperate wish for a particular phenomenon or result to occur. This wish fills you with dread that the opposite might occur and befuddles your prophetic acuity. When your mind subsequently receives the right answer, your dread refuses to accept it. And so, you predict *not* what your psychic power center perceived, but what you *wish* it had perceived.

2. LACK OF OBJECTIVITY. Too much knowledge of

the wrong kind about what you are trying to predict, or knowledge of a misleading nature, or of a kind that appeals to you most, will blind you to the truth of what your psychic power center perceives. Without your even trying to, as a result, you tend to mold the psychic impression you receive about it into what you presume it *ought* to be logically. As a consequence, you predict *not* what your psychic power center "received," but what you assume it *ought* to have received.

3. OVERRESPONSE TO SUGGESTION. Suggestions by others either in writing (as from the media or in a letter), or orally (as from a speech or a conversation), or telepathically (as from another person's wish thinking), or in sympathy (as from your own emotions, pity, sense of justice, fervent desire to help the other person, and the like) will saturate your psychic power center and alter the color of the prediction you receive in order to "fit it in with" the suggestion itself, or to try to make the prediction come to pass.

4. STATE OF YOUR HEALTH. You predict most accurately when you are healthy and free of pain. That's why in my latest psychic discovery book, *Somo-Psychic Power: Using Its Miracle Forces for a Fabulous New Life,* I teach the reader how to feel at his healthiest, so he can extract the utmost hidden power from his psychic power center. When you are in fine health and free of pain, you are at your most objective, at your most courageous to face the worst, and you are then less affected by tremulous wish thinking and less responsive to suggestion. Your sympathetic and parasympathetic nervous systems (your yang and yin) are perfectly balanced then, and you leave your conscious and subconscious minds less subject to one-sided emotion.

You are affected just the opposite when gripped with pain, terror of the future, discomfort, incapacity, and other sequelae of sickness, disease, or even of undiagnosable chronic health problems. All these plagues super-sensitize your mind to the least impressions, particularly to those which comfort or flatter your ego and distort the accuracy of the predictions you receive.

5. MUSCLE TONE. To be healthy but without muscle

tone is akin to being naturally intelligent but without the education to use it. Muscle tone reinforces the courage in your brain by adding the suggestion of a great physical power to back it up.

You feel much stronger than you really are, after all, when you contract your pectoral (chest or breast) muscles when you face trouble or disaster, than if you don't. When your "aggressive" muscles are maintained naturally toned, your whole body automatically backs up your psychic power (and your conscious and subconscious minds as well) *reflexly,* with the independent feeling that you *can* stand on your own feet, come what may. When any prophecy is triggered in your psychic power center, you then normally accept it like a philosopher, no matter what side it favors, and present it as it is, with the least distortion.

People who fail to predict with accuracy are usually handicapped by one of these five lacks. My Zohar Science courses and books are designed to overcome them and release your psychic powers in full.

Of what do your Zohar Science courses consist?

YOUNG: They are provided by mail by Clarion, and they are designed for the everyday application of psychic power for self-advancement, social and romantic goals, and for the transformation of one into the most effective person he wishes to be. Although the courses may be enjoyable for idle pastime, they are prepared for *achievement* in every phase of life. And they do not require scientific instruments, talismans, tormenting postures, fasting, or any other similar self-sacrifice or additional expense. They depend only on one's psychic power center and the Zohar Science secrets.

You will still refuse to accept offers to lecture, go on radio or television?

YOUNG: I certainly will!

—13

Exploring Frontiers
of the Spirit

"SPIRITUAL FRONTIERS FELLOWSHIP, INC., is a national organization, non-denominational, founded in Chicago on March 5, 1956, by laymen and clergymen active in the major Christian denominations of the United States. The fellowship was chartered under the laws of the state of Illinois as a religious, non-profit corporation. In the words of its constitution, Spiritual Frontiers Fellowship was established 'to sponsor, explore, and interpret the growing interest in psychic phenomena and mystical experience within the Church, wherever these experiences relate to effective prayer, spiritual healing, and personal survival. The fellowship has as its goal the development of spiritual growth in the individual and the encouragement of new dimensions of spiritual experience within the Church.' It is Christian in origin and emphasis, interdenominational in scope, and interfaith in pursuit of its ultimate goal."—[*Spiritual Frontiers Fellowship*]

The National Headquarters of Spiritual Frontiers Fellowship (SFF), at 800 Custer Avenue in Evanston, issues a quarterly journal and maintains a lending library for members. Most members of the fellowship are also active participants in orthodox church communities. They find no contradiction in belief structures, nor do they suffer doctrinal trauma. It is, in fact, part of the avowed purpose of SFF to enlarge the conventional churches' "interpretation of the Old and New Testament heritage" and encourage them to "recapture the faith and experience of the First Century in order that they may be able to speak with conviction to the Twentieth Century."

Three main areas of concern that SFF emphasizes are 1) the development of creative and mystical prayer, 2) spiritual healing, and 3) personal immortality and the eternal life of the spirit.

Although not all its members may necessarily agree with or comprehend certain of the philosophical principles and viewpoints that are the special interests of SFF, these may be listed as six basic tenets:

1. There are two worlds, which interact with one another. One is the physical world as we know it, subject to the laws of physics and biology; the other is the nonphysical or psychic world, which is just as real and emanating from the same divine Mind.

2. Man is an inhabitant of both worlds. Increased spiritual experience helps him become more aware of his true heritage as a child of God with unlimited potential for growth.

3. The Bible, and more specifically the New Testament, offers a reliable report of men and women dealing with the spiritual world. SFF accepts the benefits of modern technology, but it calls upon its members not to demythologize the Gospels by abstracting from them the supernatural elements.

4. SFF is part of a general revolt against nineteenth-century materialism and believes that all human experiences, in-

cluding psi abilities, are to be studied without prejudice for a better understanding of the invisible world and the true nature of man and the universe.

5. SFF maintains that a valid, personal relationship with the spiritual world enables contemporary man to better understand the human problems of suffering, injustice, and death.

6. SFF believes that God still speaks to man and that the doors of revelation are never closed.

On May 23, 24, and 25, 1974, I was pleased to participate in the SFF Annual Conference at Chicago's Bismarck Hotel by presenting a workshop on the revelatory experience. During the conference, the Reverend J. Gordon Melton arranged for me to conduct an informal panel with certain very articulate and well-informed spokesmen of Spiritual Frontiers Fellowship. These members were Rev. Paul Lambourne Higgins, cofounder of SFF and its first president; Rev. Ross K. Sweeny, a past president of SFF; William G. Boykin, executive director, Texas Press Association; Norlan Kemp, lay healer-counselor; Nancy French, psychic counselor-teacher; and Carol Douglas, registered nurse-healer.

Was there any difficulty seeking an identity in the early days of SFF, or did the very fine precepts, which I find so beautifully stated on the inside covers of each issue of the journal, become crystallized at once?

REV. ROSS K. SWEENY: A lot of prayer went into SFF. There had previously been formed, a couple of years prior, our sister organization in Great Britain. Some people who had a hunger for this wanted to start a counterpart in this country, then they selected the name—Spiritual Frontiers. We're exploring frontiers of the spirit. We feel that SFF is a fellowship made up of those who believe in one or more of our purposes. We feel sometimes that the name has unfortunate implications, because some people do not understand the meaning of the word "spiritual." They confuse it with "Spiritualism," and SFF has nothing to do with it. Quite often, someone will think SFF is a Spiritualist church, and this has been an unfortunate thing.

At the same time, you would not close the door to a Spirit-

ualist medium becoming a member of Spiritual Frontiers or participating in Spiritual Frontiers.

REVEREND SWEENY: We could not be true to our own heritage of being pioneers out here on the frontier if we closed any doors. We think that our mission is to open doors.

REV. PAUL LAMBOURNE HIGGINS: While we were founded on the basic idea of reinteresting and revitalizing the Christian churches, we have always kept open to other groups and other believers. There are Jews within the fellowship; there are those from the Eastern religions; and there are those from the small, independent sects. We feel that the basic things which Christianity stands for are prevalent, in some measure at least, in the other religions of the world. We recognize that there is a universality here and that Christ says, "I have sheep of other pastures."

So you would not tell someone that he could not truly become a member of SFF until he accepted Jesus as his personal Saviour.

REVEREND HIGGINS: No, we definitely would not say that. We really feel that the great Christ, whom we recognize as our Saviour, the Virgin's very son, is much, much greater than that, and that God makes himself known in other ways and to other people. It's the same Christ, the same Virgin Mary, the same Isis, the same Demeter, the same eternal God, who speaks to us under different names. This is really how I feel about it.

Reverend Higgins, could you as co-founder of SFF tell us more about the early days of organization?

REVEREND HIGGINS: All in all, I feel, Brad, that the concepts have remained the same. We have kept pretty much to the same basic things. There's been a lot of progress.

When we first got under way, in 1956, a few of us had been talking about these things and keeping in communication on the possibilities of getting a fellowship under way within the churches—something that might be done to study the psychical, mystical manifestations in the churches as these things relate to prayer and healing and immortality. Margueritte Bro, and her husband, the late Alvin Bro, were two who were very instrumental in this, along with Arthur Ford, and Alston Smith, George Wright, and Sherwood Eddy.

When I was pastor at Hyde Park Methodist Church, near the campus, University of Chicago, we decided that we really ought to proceed into something. We sent out an invitation to the different ones with whom we had been in correspondence, and certain others all over the country. Almost a hundred people came, from the Atlantic coast to the Pacific coast to Chicago, just to get together to talk about these things. We had a good program, too, with several good speakers. At the conclusion, we formed the Spritual Frontiers Fellowship, and I was elected first president.

The purpose of SFF, as we defined it, was that it would be for the study of mystical and psychical experiences, especially within the churches and as they relate to effective prayer and meditation, to spiritual healing, and to personal immortality. We got a library organized; we saw some study groups formed, area chairmen named, and a journal put out; and the fellowship began to move ahead.

It was a little more difficult in those days than today, because this wasn't particularly popular in the churches. But it was all good. We felt really called to this, and we've been very happy for the most part with the development through the years. Sometimes when a group grows, it gets bigger, gets out of hand, and other emphases come into the picture; but I think for the most part that we've kept pretty much to the basic principles with which we started.

As a clergyman, don't you feel a tragic kind of loss that the Church has lost sight of some of these gifts of the spirit? Even today, with such movements as Spiritual Frontiers, and with the great kind of spiritual awareness that's going on, I think far too many orthodox congregations feel, or at least infer, that their minister may not himself believe in survival, spiritual healing, or effective prayer.

REVEREND HIGGINS: Well, this has been our concern from the very beginning, that the churches were not being true to their original purpose. The churches were founded to spread the gospel. The gospel is good news, good news about eternal life, the whole resurrection concept. This was the thing that the saints stressed; this was the thing that the Church in its greatest days of faith wholly stressed. And when the Church loses this, it's lost its real mission.

We were all confident that the Church's purposes are directed in this direction, toward a revival of spiritual interest, and it just needed to be done. The churches had become interested in all the social and political activities—all having their place—but had really lost touch with the spiritual springs of life.

Although we use the term "orthodox" in different ways, we almost feel that we in SFF are orthodox, because we're trying to recover what was originally expressed in the Apostles' Creed.

REVEREND SWEENY: When Spiritual Frontiers was begun, we began with the idea of being a servant of the Church, at the same time feeling that the Church had lost certain emphases that were basic in the early Christian Church. If we do our job properly, the Church once again will become acquainted with these emphases and be the church it intended to be under the direction of the Holy Spirit.

The birthday of the Church was Pentecost, when the Holy Spirit became a moving force in the Church. We feel that when we do our job effectively, we can go out of existence, because once more the Church will take over its proper job. We feel that the Church has abdicated its responsibility because of its fears and hangups in some of these things.

Spiritual Frontiers, then, wishes to show that the Church can be spiritually, as well as socially, relevant.

REVEREND SWEENY: Lay people are finding that they are being given the gifts of the spirit, such as healing, clairvoyance, clairaudience. Here is evidence of the work of the Holy Spirit. Here is a new priesthood of all believers.

The laity is now, I think, calling the pastors to accountability, and is "priesting" the pastors. This definitely is the understanding of the priesthood of all believers: I am your priest, but you are also my priest. If I am lacking, you, in the name of Christ, can priest me and call me to my duty, my obligation. Historically, the Church has always emphasized faith and works. I believe the Church has got off the track, forgetting about the faith, emphasizing the works. Some have said, "Faith without works is dead." And we have become so preoccupied with the social concerns that we have forgotten the faith which gives us the motivation and gives us the fire and gives us the impetus for it. If you do this without faith, it becomes a very sterile, barren thing. If you do it with faith and with a knowledge of the fruits of the spirit, and if you exemplify this in your life, you can share with others your love and your gratitude. When you emphasize social concerns without faith, what develops is anger, resentment, argument, debate; instead of emphasizing the fruits of the spirit, you've been emphasizing the works of the flesh.

NORLAN KEMP: The Church started losing the mystical qualities, the spiritual qualities, when science moved in and said, "This can't be true!" They put scientific guidelines to everything back in the 1800s, and scared the Church away from these things because they couldn't be proved scientifically. Churchmen backed away and listened to the scientists and said, "Well, perhaps you're right." Now that the scientists are coming back and *proving* these spiritual things, the Church is having to take another look.

REVEREND SWEENY: And the Church has been locked into a brand of science that is outdated and outmoded and is no longer acceptable as science. Scientists are now saying to churchmen, "Where we used to frighten you and scare you off, we believe that we are going to be the ones that will have to scientifically prove to you and bring you back to faith!"

Recently I saw a poster that said, "Death is Nature's way of recycling human beings." What is SFF's position on reincarnation?

WILLIAM BOYKIN: Spiritual Frontiers is not a church;

.. has no doctrine; this is our freedom. Each individual is free to believe what he wishes. Spiritual Frontiers has no position on any one of these things.

KEMP: One thing I think we should consider here is that the very word "Christ" (which was the start of the word "Christian"), traced back, actually means "spirit" in the old languages. "Spirit" being the eternal person, reincarnation, in the light of the eternal person, depends on *that* person, which is before a body life and which is after a body life. That decision is actually an individual one. Reincarnation can be for one person and not actually be for another. So it is the person's spirit, which the original meaning started out to be, which we've kind of lost in the Church today. We call ourselves Christians, and we don't really know what we're calling ourselves.

REVEREND SWEENY: The Hindu, for example, developed a caste system with reincarnation; and they're having difficulty getting rid of the caste system in India now. It was something they used to keep certain people at certain levels during their lifetime. The new Hindu, the intellectual Hindu, sees that this was misused. Gandhi saw it, made it illegal to have the caste system.

The younger Hindu is going back to reincarnation the same way the Christian is. I think that all of us are at certain levels of studying reincarnation. Some of us are saying, "All right, what was it originally? Why do we think that there must be something there that we have to know about?" As Les Farmer says, "Leave the jury out until we can determine why we've misused it." Even in the Bible, reincarnation is not properly interpreted to us in translations. Reincarnation is a new frontier for us. We have so many prejudices! Reincarnation has been misused by so many different writers and so many different denominations.

REVEREND HIGGINS: I feel reincarnation is one of the several possibilities that needs always to be kept in the picture for any objective investigator in these fields. I personally feel that reincarnation has considerable support from a biblical and a religious background, but that it's very often misunderstood.

I believe it has to be considered only a part of the picture.

While I believe in reincarnation in a certain sense, definitely, I do not accept the general idea of reincarnation as you so often hear it. I feel there are times when individuals will "flunk the course" and will have to take it over again. Therefore the people who have lived here before—some of *us* who lived here before—may be back again. But I believe that there are worlds infinitely beyond this world. I believe that life is one continuing life that embraces far, far more than just this world and all the worlds that are.

CAROL DOUGLAS: I know I have lived before; I am aware of it; but it doesn't matter, really. If I'm supposed to come back, I'll hack it. But I'm trying to do as much as I can right now, because I'm not counting on coming back again to finish up what I've started now. I'm so excited about what I'm doing, and going into, that I'm trying to complete now what I'm supposed to do, and I'm not really worried about the next life.

Would Spiritual Frontiers be enthusiastic about the kind of program they have in England, where the lay healer, faith healer, whatever term you prefer, is able to come into the hospital and work directly in conjunction with the orthodox medical staff?

KEMP: I'm doing that sort of thing now as a layman. I have taken courses through the hospital with the chaplain there, and I come in and work directly out of the emergency room, out of intensive care. At the times I work, I am the only representative of the Church in the hospital. I handle things like death, emotional shock—anything that arises while I'm there in the hospital.

About the question of guidelines, well, this is a touchy area. It is very necessary to have guidelines, to establish a license for something like this. But when you set up guidelines, you may weed out a lot of potential.

REVEREND SWEENY: And you also weed out those who want to use this for an ego trip or for a self-serving thing. Healing is to be a ministry of service. Healing is to glorify the Giver of all great gifts, rather than the one who possesses the gifts. This is where licensing would become important.

BOYKIN: We have a certified lay program in the Methodist Church, where the layman can go through certain courses and become certified as a lay speaker. I believe that a certified lay *healer* in the Methodist Church is a concept they should also adopt.

Healing is one of the gifts of the spirit, spoken of so often in the New Testament, yet how many churches have a healing service as a part of their regular Sunday activities?

KEMP: I think that so far as a break-through in the Church—healing is probably the number one possibility that could be most easily accepted. However, many people still have hangups on it. And I have observed that if an individual has certain hangups or certain limitations, that he can only be comfortable in an area that is compatible with his hangups.

BOYKIN: If we can get Spiritual Frontiers Fellowship to be the certification group, healing would be under the umbrella of a religious organization, a mixture of the laity with the clergy. There are certification programs for all types of groups —public accountants, life underwriters in insurance. . . . If we can start a certification program, we can write the guidelines. This does not mean we would eliminate those who didn't go through the SFF certification program, but we would be the first in this country to have it.

REVEREND SWEENY: Bill, I think, mentioned one very important point when he said this is not just for ministers, but for laity as well. We need to reclaim our spiritual heritage; and the laity and the clergy can do this. The Holy Spirit can work through anyone who is willing to be used.

BOYKIN: I've watched state legislatures for twenty years, and all these various groups come in to be licensed. They bring their own laws; they bring their own regulations. I want to have our laws prepared, so that we can go to the state capitols and say, "These are the guidelines for our certification programs." I don't think we want licensing; we'd like to stay outside of that. In England they have accredited, certified healers in various areas; and I see this coming in this country. And part of my role in this is to look at the legislative problems that we're going to have in all the states.

Carol, as a nurse, have you been able to use spiritual healing in the hospitals?

MS. DOUGLAS: Yes, yes, all the time.

Do you have approbation or disapprobation from your superiors?

MS. DOUGLAS: I don't talk about it; I just do it.

How do you do it in that kind of structure?

MS. DOUGLAS: Oh, I can do laying on of hands any time, and I do it *all* the time.

Is the patient aware of what you're doing?

MS. DOUGLAS: Sometimes. When I'm working with the retarded, I can't reach them on a verbal level; so the healing works because I'm reaching them on a non-verbal level. You can just call it love. As you work, you're loving them, and you're appealing to whatever intelligence there is there that can't communicate normally.

Psychotics will quiet right down, put the chair down, and talk to you. The retarded will relax and let you take care of them. They'll work up to their optimum. The physical pain goes away, and the temperature goes down.

I haven't had any luck that I can see with the retardation itself, but their fear goes away. And they respond as much as they're able to respond. I'm working now trying to find out what I can do to tune up, to help with the retardation itself.

I was in surgery for nine years; and there, the spirit is always present. The body is asleep, but the spirit is right there; and you can communicate on a non-verbal level. The spirit, the essence that's there, knows that you're helping. It's very interested in what's going on, so long as it knows you're helping and knows that you're not afraid.

Then, the chemically induced state of sleep permits you greater contact, almost as if it were a trance state, so that you can communicate more effectively?

MS. DOUGLAS: Yes, the patient is separated from what's going on in his body; yet he's very interested—and usually very afraid.

He knows that he has no control over that body. There's a

Exploring Frontiers of the Spirit

fear that comes with lack of control. And if the patients hook up with me and realize that I'm not afraid, then they borrow my confidence. The body relaxes; blood pressure is normal; bleeding is minimized; trauma is minimized. There's a terrific trauma just from holding someone's body open; they've never felt air in there before!

Don't you wish you could come out of the closet, so to speak?

MS. DOUGLAS: Every time I do, I wish I hadn't. There are some who realize what I'm doing, some who work with me and who really enjoy it. Each place where I've worked, there have been a couple of doctors who are hungry to know about it, and who work right with it.

But other doctors don't want to hear anything about it. Maybe they've tried it and been rebuffed. So I usually decide I'm not going to say anything. But I'm working all the time, whether I say anything or not.

Don't you think that any successful doctor is a healer on the spiritual, as well as the physical, level, whether he is aware of it or not?

MS. DOUGLAS: Oh, certainly! When you move close to a surgeon—when you're in surgery you're about as close as you're going to get—you can feel it! Those who are in tune, you work right with them. Those are the cases where you don't have to say anything. Whatever he needs, you've got in your hand. It's beautiful.

Why don't general practitioners touch people more?

MS. DOUGLAS: They're afraid to. They're shy, some of them, and some of them don't like to touch people.

It's a beautiful thing for one human being to be able to reach out and touch another.

NANCY FRENCH: Yes, but, then, in counseling or in healing with a man—because I wear a female body—I look to see first whether or not a man can afford to have me touch him. Even some women, you know, have a fear of homosexuality, and so they have this "Please don't touch me; talk to me!"

KEMP: Some women are afraid to have a man touch them in healing.

One thing I have found helpful in the healing ministry—if I do not know a person—is to say, "Will you place my hands where the pain is?" If they do it themselves, this is accceptable.

MS. FRENCH: And they are exerting some control. Sometimes I announce my intent by saying, "I'm going to touch your body now, right here."

Or "Do you want me to?" thus making that verbal bridge so that they take a responsibility in deciding whether or not they want to be touched. Somebody in the healing group yesterday—a woman—jumped back from me. I asked, "Do you want me to touch you?" She really made about as much of a jump as I've ever seen anybody make. She said, "No, definitely not!"

The beautiful thing about the various gifts of the spirit is that, while mystical in origin, they are so very practical, so very useful to man on the earth plane.

REVEREND HIGGINS: Yes, because the mystical *is* very practical. It's the life of God in the soul. If we sense the mystical that way, if we get into the harmony of it, life begins to become meaningful and we move toward wholeness. The mystical is practical. It makes for the good life; it makes for what Jesus calls the abundant life.

Spiritual Frontiers publishes a number of principles in its journal—and I agree with those principles—but would you say that Spiritual Frontiers also has dogma?

REVEREND HIGGINS: Well, we hope always to keep it as a fellowship, and not as anything that would resemble it being another church. We have tried to keep away from dogma. I suppose if there is any dogma, it would simply be that we really do believe in the effectiveness of real prayer and meditation in spiritual healing, and in the psychical evidences and personal experiences that relate to life after death. We really do believe in these things. So maybe this is dogmatic in one sense, yet we want to keep open to explore.

And Spiritual Frontiers Fellowship was organized in Psychic Chicago!

REVEREND SWEENY: Chicago is the theological capital of the world. The theological seminaries are quite uninformed about this whole area; and we feel, since they are places for the training of ministers, that this is a real tragedy. If SFF can be resource people for these seminaries, we can be of tremendous service in helping to train ministers to be able to minister to the total man. We feel we are in a strategic spot here in Chicago to be of service to the Church at large.

KEMP: There's an old saying about Chicago being a city of change. The people here are a very strong people, and they can handle changes with a facility that I've not seen in other parts of the country. Other cities seem more reluctant to try on something new. The people here are willing to take a look at something, try it; and if it fits, they use it!

REVEREND HIGGINS: Yes, and it could be the old concept that some spiritual power exists right here in this area. I feel there is such a power in certain sections of the world.

It is interesting that Chicago, theologically, has the major seminaries here. A great deal has come out of the Chicago seminaries in regard to archaeology, history, comparative religion—these subjects that all have a relationship to what we're talking about.

Whether there is a spiritual aura, a spiritual power impregnating this very part of the world like we will certainly find in holy places in Europe, like at the Cathedral at Chartres and Glastonbury Abbey, and so on, I don't know; but something has been in the background, I believe, in drawing people here.

What is the role of Spiritual Frontiers in the New Age?

REVEREND SWEENY: Well, the thing I see really at this point would be like "future shock." People are not prepared spiritually to handle all these changes coming about. One very real area for Spiritual Frontiers is to help people bridge these gaps; in other words, to make stable areas where people can get a firm foundation.

MS. FRENCH: I think what SFF is working toward, as far as a threshold, is to help people to be free enough to balance the spiritual life with their daily living life.

Teaching men and women to walk in balance.

MS. FRENCH: Yes, walk in balance. And this goes into your molecular structure. Anything that's going wrong, so to speak, or going right, is because of the molecular structure of that which exists on another level. SFF, I think, is working in that area.

REVEREND HIGGINS: The Spiritual Frontiers Fellowship role it seems to me, is twofold at this point: first, to conserve all that is good out of our heritage of the past, and to build upon the best of the past; secondly, to look ahead to the future with an openness to new revelations. "I have other things to say to you that you cannot bear now," Jesus said. I think we need to be awake to that. I believe that then we will see more of a universal concept of religious truth being accepted that will lift all of us out of some of the narrowness and some of the bigotry that have too often been destructive.

It's a very important time for Spiritual Frontiers to keep the balance—appreciation of the past, possibilities for the future—and to help move ahead into new frontiers that are really not new, except that they are new to us.

MS. DOUGLAS: Spiritual Frontiers is teaching us to get in tune with God and our own deeper, inner, better selves—our Over-Self, you might call it. When we learn to do that, then we can do whatever we have to do, and handle whatever changes in the world come along. We have the security of knowing that, no matter what happens, we're in tune; and we may be the ones who can help to keep other people from going under. When we are strong with a strength that is not our own, we can help the ones who are around us. And we'd better be ready!

Exploring Frontiers of the Spirit

—14

New Age Chicago

THE STELLE COMMUNITY, which now consists of about 280 members, apprehends the current recession as the beginning of a series of cataclysmic disasters that will continue for the remainder of the century. Economic chaos, earth changes, a series of world wars will culminate in Armageddon in May 2000.

Richard Kieninger first shared his vision of the end time in his biography, *The Ultimate Frontier,* published in 1963. Kieninger tells how a mysterious Dr. White appeared to him as a child and delineated not only who Richard had been in former lives, but what his mission was to be in his present lifetime. Dr. White revealed that Kieninger must establish a community of resourceful men and women who would be prepared to build a better world after Armageddon decimates earth's population in the years 2000 and 2001.

Stelle (German for "place") is now located in Ford County, a hundred miles south of Chicago. The community was established as a private corporation by Richard and Gail Kieninger in 1973. While other communities across the United States are struggling against the hard times with varying degrees of despair, the residents of Stelle see recessions, depressions, and wars and rumors of wars as part of a great master plan.

"If you think you know why you're here and where you're going, it makes it easier," Gail Kieninger told United Press International reporter Pamela Reeves. "It takes the fear out of it.

"We're not waiting for the Apocalypse. It very rarely comes up in conversation. If it doesn't come off, then what do we lose? We'll just be better prepared for living. We'll still have Stelle."

It has been often stated that great events cast their shadows before them, and hundreds of visionary men and women have perceived a very great shadow blocking an orderly view of the future. Whether one terms the coming great event Judgment Day, the Time of Great Cleansing, the Period of Purification, a Time of Transition, really makes little difference. According to the predictions of Edgar Cayce and his contemporary seers, the ancient predictions of Amerindian medicine people, certain interpreters of the Bible, and a good many scientists who make logical extensions of the current state of affairs blighting planet earth, something very heavy is, indeed, about to "come off."

The Foundation Church of the Millennium, 1529 North Wells Street, believes that God will send a Messiah "to lead His people out of the dark times of 'the end' to a 'New Beginning' (seen in the Bible as the Millennium) where civilization will prosper under spiritual authority."

A pamphlet distributed by the Foundation Church states: "One of the greatest problems of today is the void of leadership in the world. And we believe that a Messiah will indeed come; not as some supernatural being, but as someone with the qualities of leadership which will inspire his people to a new way of living."

Father Lucius, a Foundation Church spokesman, told me:

"We believe that to every human being there is a God-self, or higher self, and this is what we encourage in that we see this element of each individual as that which has contact with God."

The Foundation Church assesses its current function as being able to provide "spiritual and moral leadership, by asserting and affirming the values and codes in which we believe, by helping and supporting people in need, by offering a cause and a purpose for those looking for meaning in their lives and searching for truth within themselves."

"I think the current lack of stability in society is ultimately serving a positive purpose by bringing an acute interest in the spiritual to the fore," Father Nathan remarked during my requested interview with a representative from the Foundation Church. "Material values are proving insufficient. Human systems are breaking down. It is one of the basic essentials of our belief and the teachings of the Foundation Church that the world as we know it is ending. The Messianic Age, or the New Age, is close at hand, in the year 2000.

"I feel that mankind is about to take a great leap forward in his spiritual evolution," Father Nathan went on, "but whether or not all of mankind is ready to participate in that leap is another thing. I think a lot of people are going to be in for a big shock—which may be their undoing or their salvation, depending on how they respond to it. I think there is a turning point coming, a cyclic end of an age; and those who attune themselves to the new requirements will be able to make the transition, to move into a new consciousness, a God-consciousness.

"Chicago is a power center. And with all power coming from God, that makes the city significant. Energy, love, and creativity are here. We feel that being in Chicago and being a part of the vibes of Chicago puts us in a good position to affect large numbers of people.

"I believe that there are spiritual nodal points throughout the world. There are areas of spiritual intensity, vortexes of energy through which come spiritual insight, revelation. There *are* holy places.

"Now, in many ways Chicago is a decidedly *un*holy place; but there is a particular kind of vortex here, an energy, that brings people together on a spiritual level.

"I see the New Age, personally, as a time of return to a very basic harmony with the Earth and with Heaven. The atmosphere in Chicago makes it an in-between point. It is a great mass of people, rather than a cosmopolitan center. It's not a city like New York is a city. Chicago is really a very large small town, without the impersonality and restrictions of a large city. There is still a feeling of being in touch with the earth here.

"Again, my vision of the New Age is, you know, swords into ploughshares, spears into pruning hooks—a harmonious relationship with the earth. I feel that Chicago will offer a link between an industrialized megalopolis and a very agrarian, earth-centered life."

Rev. Orchid Neal was another who viewed the troubled times of the transitional period in a positive light: "Now is the most exciting time to live. Of all the things and all the events that have occurred in the past, today is one of the most exciting stages of our spiritual evolution.

"I feel that something very dramatic and traumatic is about to happen. I feel that there will be changes on the surface of the earth itself. There is evidence that our climate is changing already.

"I feel that Chicago will possibly be the main center of spiritual activity in the New Age."

Joanne Ernast foresees certain people of New Age spirit forming a circle of light in Chicago. "I know that, in Atlantis, the power crystals were hidden before the time of destruction. There is one amongst us in Chicago who knows where the crystals are hidden. If my memory serves me, there are seven who must come together so that the crystals can be totally activated. So far as I know, only two have definitely come together."

"If you believe in reincarnation," Vanessa Whitlock told me, "you know that the people who once walked this land on this very spot are returning. There have been many, many colo-

New Age Chicago

nizations on this planet, one of which was in the area of Chicago.

"Yes, there was an ancient civilization here. It had nothing to do with the American Indians or their ancestors. These were people of another time, another place. Now their souls have returned to this vibratory place whereon the city of Chicago has been built. Their memory locks are being triggered. These returning entities and the vibrations here on this site together make up Psychic Chicago."

Past-life reader Kathleen Fry said that in addition to "meeting" so many people from the court of Louis XIV, she picks up vibrations that Chicago was built on the site of a city that was pre-Atlantean. "This area was under water during the end days of Atlantis. This was a flourishing city *before* the great days of Atlantis. I see that the entities who lived here were taller, more slender, than either us or the Atlanteans. Their skin is not what we would call white, but rather a light gray."

I asked Kathleen what kind of past lives she picked up for most of the active, practicing psychics in Chicago.

"I really don't get any single kind of pattern," she replied. "Most of them seem to have some connection either with the practicing of alchemy or the founding of universities in the thirteenth and early-fourteenth centuries. They generally led religious, contemplative lives."

Are they incarnating at this specific time in order to help people get through the time of transition?

"Yes," Kathleen said after a moment's hesitation, "but one of things that I've picked up is an intense curiosity to see what the end time of this period, this 'end of the world' will be like. Many of them have gone through end times before. Some have been here for catastrophe after catastrophe. Everyone seems to want to be back for this. Especially those who had to do with the death of Atlantis."

Such talk of reincarnation, the ring of return, cyclic ends of ages, and patterns of entities coming back to once again undergo transition periods led me to John Cejka, the president of Cyclomatic Engineering, Inc., of Glenview, Illinois. Cejka and his associates devote enormous amounts of time to studying cycles, especially those concerned with weather energy. The accuracy of their work has enabled them to make astoundingly accurate predictions. The intellectual lodestone of Cyclomatic Engineering was mined in the 1930s by two brilliant scientists, Dr. Selby Maxwell and Dr. Raymond Wheeler.

JOHN CEJKA: Dr. Wheeler discovered a hundred-year cycle, which is divided into four almost equal parts, that demonstrates that man has behaved differently—but *predictably*—during periods of warm-wet, warm-dry, cold-wet, and cold-dry weather. Wars, depressions, revolutions, cataclysmic events, and changes in the height of hemlines have occurred at evenly spaced intervals.

Astronomer Selby Maxwell, once science editor of the Chicago *Tribune,* discovered a weather-energy cycle which has proved to be the *basic cycle* which governs *all* weather—past, present, and future. Maxwell determined the correct time lags which cause the turbulent upper-air masses to act in a predetermined manner. Essential to Maxwell's method for predicting the weather was his revelation that *all cycles of the same length turn at the same time and that all cycles are related in one way or another to this basic energy cycle.*

The Maxwell-Wheeler discoveries of weather-energy cycles and human ecology give us a roadmap of time. We are not simply talking about when it will rain or snow. We are stating that the weather, the waging of war, the price of commodities, the length of hair over the ears, every single enterprise and endeavor of man has its own cycle. All these cycles, in turn, are interrelated and affected by the basic energy cycle.

So you are stating that once man recognizes that patterns of time do recur at rhythmic intervals, he can chart danger periods for his government, plan ahead for droughts and famines, and attempt to stockpile goods for periods of depression and inflation.

CEJKA: yes, and the Maxwell-Wheeler curves also

New Age Chicago

parallel, and thereby preview, the stock-market fluctuations. Business cycles have been integrated with weather trends and cultural patterns throughout history. The Maxwell Weather-Energy Cycle and the Wheeler Culture Curve combine to provide an infalliable predictor of the business cycles of all nations.

What can the Maxwell-Wheeler roadmap of time tell us about what lies in store for us?

CEJKA: Dr. Wheeler found that at the end of every other five-hundred-year cycle there are major revolutions which occur over the entire world and which result in drastic reorganizations of society. According to his projections, we are in a revolution of this sort now, comparable to the collapse of medieval culture and the beginning of the Modern world.

Wheeler also foresaw a great renaissance, which will be due at the end of the century. This collective rebirth will involve the great masses of the people participating in the economic and political structures to an extent unknown before in history.

The main divisions of history—ancient, medieval, and modern—serve also as landmarks in the history of world climate, Wheeler said. "Old civilizations collapse and new civilizations are born on tides of climatic change. The turning points occur when cold-dry times reach maximum severity."

Those of us who are living today are entering a cold-dry period and are witnessing a time of revolution. Before our eyes, an old world is dying and a new one is being born. Those of us who will be alive at the termination of this coming time of famine, revolution, depression, and the collapse of the old civilization will witness the advent of a new Renaissance, a surge of renewed life force, a restructured political and economic viability.

Out of the reshuffling, the chaos, the societal confusion, will come a renaissance in about the year 2000. The turning point will come sometime in the 1980s. Right now, according to the research of Raymond Wheeler, we are living at a time comparable to 1480, just before the advent of the great Renaissance of 1500.

The decline of an old world, such as we are experiencing

in the next few decades, is always characterized by a succession of rapidly occurring and troublesome depressions. Prosperity, as we have known it, is due to decline for an extended period. Times may have changed from the earlier terminations of five hundred-year cycles, but the laws of nature have not. Difficult times have occurred in each of the twenty-six preceding cold-dry phases of the hundred-year cycle. We are now entering the twenty-seventh cold-dry phase since 575 B.C. Although we cannot expect any different treatment from the recurrent cycle, we do have some knowledge of how to prepare ourselves.

Remarkably, in the combined work of two brilliant scientists we have been given a preview of the last twenty-five years of our century which completely echoes the "Earth Changes" material of Edgar Cayce, the Amerindian prophecies of a Time of Great Purification, the interpretation many fundamentalist Christians place on apocalyptic passages in the biblical book of *Revelation,* and the impressions of those sensitives who reside in Psychic Chicago.

We have been told, according to the extensive research of Wheeler and Maxwell, that a study of historical cycles indicates that we are in the midst of a world convulsion second only to the emergence of rational thought in the sixth century B.C., the fall of Rome and other ancient civilizations in the fifth century A.D., and the Renaissance after the collapse of the Middle Ages. The Maxwell-Wheeler Weather-Energy Cycle warns us to prepare for colder weather and for long periods of drought, which will, of course, result in scarcity of food for the prosperous nations, famine for the poorer countries.

These convulsions of a dying world will last until the end of the century. "Remember, though," John Cejka offers by way of encouragement, "civilization has survived four great convulsions since ancient times comparable to the one we are now entering. Each time, the world has emerged better than it was before—more stable, richer, with greater concern for the worth of the individual."

"I feel that we are truly on the verge of a New Age,"

Henry Rucker said to me. "Surely the ecumenical spirit of the churches has got to be one of the beginnings of the transition. And I think that science is going to move gradually to the side of metaphysics. Physicians are going to become more metaphysical, too. I can see the day when a doctor has done all that he can for you, and he tells you to go see your God.

"I would say that if we receive a sudden advancement into the New Age, it will come about because of a real manifestation of what we now call 'space beings.' I think our evolution in true awareness involves the recognition of life on other worlds, other dimensions. We've got to see that we are just a little cell in this fantastic cosmic body!"

When New Age consciousness has truly permeated the hearts and minds of those who have managed the transition to the renaissance world of 2000, I predict that one of the most influential power places will be Psychic Chicago, doorway to another dimension of being and awareness.

APPENDIX

The Chicago Psychic/Metaphysical/Occult/New Age Community: A Directory and Guide
compiled by Dr. J. Gordon Melton

There is within the metropolitan Chicago area a discernible subcultural community which can for lack of a better word be termed "psychic." It is defined by its participation in "paranormal" phenomena, though that participation comes in many ways and levels. It is a "community" in that the same people tend to float among the various groupings within the community in a search for "Truth."

It will be the purpose of this directory-guide to list the key elements in this community, and to show how it is structured in Chicago (Cook County) and those counties in Illinois directly adjacent to Cook. In actuality, the Chicago psychic community includes Milwaukee and Gary-Hammond, but the latter have been excluded because of space limitations. Addresses within Chicago proper have only a zip-code number. Phones have been too ephemeral to list; check the local books for correct listings.*

* The idea of a psychic directory of Chicago grew out of a scholarly desire by its compiler to know more about the make-up and structure of what appears to be a distinct subculture in American society as a whole. To accomplish this goal, a complete directory (as far as possible) has been assembled. There has been no cutting of groups or individuals because they were considered less than the best representatives of the community. Hence, in *no* case should a listing be taken as a recommen-

I. Psychical Research

In the late 1960s, Chicago emerged as a major center of psychical research, with two colleges offering courses. The city has also been a center for social-historical research, and houses the national headquarters of the Academy of Religion and Psychical Research. The neglect of insights of the disciplines of sociology, history, and theology has been a major weakness in formal parapsychology. All the individuals listed below are available for lectures for outside organizations and groups.

Psychology Department, Northeastern Illinois University, 5500 N. Saint Louis Avenue, 60625. Offers credit courses in parapsychology as part of an expanding interdisciplinary program. Instructors include Dr. Victor Dufour and William J. Pizzi.

Illinois Center for Parapsychological Research, 183 Grissom Lane, Hoffman Estates, 60172. Regularly brings together Chicago-area researchers, and works in co-operation with Governor's State University. The latter is building a large collection of psychic/occult literature.

Academy of Religion and Psychical Research, c/o Dr. J. Gordon Melton, Box 1311, Evanston, 60201. National body of both religious and psychical scholars.

Mundelein College, 6363 N. Sheridan Road, 60626. Offers courses in experimental parapsychology. Contact Mr. John Bisaha, Department of Psychology.

Illinois Society for Psychical Research, P.O. Box 4531, 60680

Association of Independent Psi Research Organizations, c/o Mr. Michael R. Zaeske, Box 105, Deerfield, 60015

Institute for the Study of American Religion, c/o Dr. J. Gordon Melton, Director, Box 1311, Evanston, 60201. Research on alter-

---

dation of the person or group listed, or as an endorsement of any claims that they might make. Especially does this hold for readers.

The Psychic Community is a community in constant flux. New leaders, particularly readers, arise almost weekly. This directory includes those who were known to be active as of the summer of 1975, and for whom an address or phone number could be located. We apologize for any omissions.

This directory could not have been compiled without the help of numerous people, including especially David Techter, Elinora Jaksto, Joe East, Kay Fry, and Marilyn Holmberg.

native religious bodies concentrates on metaphysical, psychical, and occult groups.

INDIVIDUAL RESEARCHERS

Mr. David Techter, P.O. Box 362, Highland Park, 60035

Fr. Richard Woods, 1143 W. North Shore Avenue, 60626

Humanistic psychology has emerged as a major focus of the psychic in the intellectual community. In Chicago, the Midwest AHP and Oasis are the most active of the several groups.

Midwest Association for Humanistic Psychology, c/o Vin Rosenthal, 815 Indian Road, Glenview, 60025

All the Way House, 1507 S. Stewart Avenue, Lombard, 60148

Analytical Psychology Club of Chicago, 3200 N. Lake Shore Drive (※807), 60657

Awareness Center, 120 S. Riverside Plaza (Suite 2166), 60606

C. G. Jung Institute of Chicago, 3200 N. Lake Shore Drive, 60657

Foundation Growth Center, 12700 Southwest Highway, Palos Park, 60464

Gestalt Institute of Chicago, 609 Davis Street, Evanston, 60201

Human Resource Developers, Inc., 112 W. Oak Street, 60610

Institute for Human Sciences, c/o Dr. Norman S. Don, Dir. of Research, 122 W. Oak Street, 60610. Wide program includes a biofeedback clinic.

Logos Institute, c/o Dr. Philip Anderson, 5757 S. University Avenue, 60637

Oasis, 12 E. Grand Avenue, 60611

Oasis North, 7463 N. Sheridan Road, 60626

A Place for Human Understanding, 5850 N. Lincoln, 60059

II. Psychic and Spiritual Groups

The psychic community in Chicago is built around numerous groups and organizations which focus activity. Those listed below are ones which offer a variety of opportunities for involvement. SFF and ARE are the largest by far.

Spiritual Frontiers Fellowship, 800 Custer Avenue, Evanston, 60202. Besides the national headquarters, there are four area groups and numerous study groups. Membership is focused in the Church.

Association for Research and Enlightenment, 1433 W. Sherwin Av-

enue, 60626. Affiliated with the national Edgar Cayce organization. It has several suburban centers and numerous groups.
Aquarian Age Psychic Center, 3253 N. Pulaski Road, 60641
Biofeedback Training Center, 125 W. Hubbard Street, 60610
Channel One, 21470 Main Street, Matteson, 60443
Chicago Ghost Tours, P.O. Box 29054, 60629
Chicago Psychic Foundation for Truth, 451 South Boulevard, Oak Park, 60302
College of Occult Studies, 505 N. Michigan Avenue, 60611
Concept Therapy Institute, c/o Lilyan Martin, 1829 W. Larchmont Avenue, 60613; or C. F. Wittenberger, 910 Hinman Avenue, Evanston, 60202
Deon's Psychic Research Center, Box 3845, Merchandise Mart, 60654
ESP Interest Group of the North Shore Unitarian Church, c/o Lori Hagler, 1219 Ridge Road, Highland Park, 60035
ESP Parties and Enterprises, c/o Mort Shenker (phone 677-4567)
Goddess Athena Reader and Advisor Ltd., c/o Christos E. Euthimious, 4750 N. Washtenaw Avenue, 60625
The Golden Path, c/o Irene Hughes, 500 N. Michigan Avenue, 60611
The Group Foundation for ESP, c/o Joe East, Box 5863, 60680
Hugh G. Carruthers Foundation, P.O. Box 460, Libertyville, 60048
Institute for Advanced Perception, c/o Harold Schroeppel, 719 S. Clarence Avenue, Oak Park, 60304
Institute of Mind Development, c/o Joe DeLouise, 6 E-Monroe Street, 60603
Institute of Regeneration, 1703 E. Olive Street, Arlington Heights, 60004
International Psychic Center, 180 N. La Salle Street, (Suite 3527), 60601
ISIS—In Search of Inner Serenity, 46 E. Cedar Street, 60611
Kay's Readers' Club, 32 N. State Street, 60602
Motivation Development Centre, c/o Mr. Paul Johnson, 1701 Lake (Suite 450), Glenview, 60025
New Psychic Research Center, c/o Del Larkin, 121 S. Third Street, Geneva, 60134
New Space Age Sciences, (phone 837-5828)
Para-Dimensions, 625 N. Michigan Avenue, 60611

Parapsychological Metaphysical Center, c/o Del Blair, 1315 E. 52nd Street, 60615

Pathways to Awareness, c/o Elayne Kudal, 5325 Woodland, Western Springs, 60558

PHATE, c/o David Burke, 1606 Columbia Bay Road, Villa Park, 60046

Psychic Research Association of Northern Illinois, 129 S. Olive, Mundelein, 60060

Psychic Research Foundation, Room 1820, 203 N. Wabash Avenue, 60601

Psychic Science Institute, P.O. Box 253, Prospect Heights, 60070

Serendipity Fellowship, c/o Douglas C. Hemstreet, 4917 N. Glenwood Avenue, 60640

SHARE, c/o S. Robert Lyter, 3129 W. Logan Boulevard, 60647

Silva Mind Control, c/o Richard E. Herro, Reg. Dir., 1127 S. Mannheim, Westchester, 60153

Spiritual Advisory Council, c/o Mr. Robert Ericsson, 1701 Lake (Suite 450), Glenview, 60025

Sunergos Institute, 4909 Forest Avenue, Downers Grove, 60515

Sunergos—CHGO, P.O. Box 276, Stuamword, 60103

Thresholds, 513 N. 10th, De Kalb, 60115.

TREK—The Inner Space Travel Agency, P.O. Box 204, Elmhurst, 60126

U and Universal Understanding, c/o Rev. Orchid Neal, 833 S. Humphrey Avenue, Oak Park, 60304

Universal Mind, c/o Phyllis Allen, 2111 W. Sunnyside Avenue, 60625

Universal Truth Center, c/o Irene Diamond, 1443 Schaumburg Road, Schaumburg, 60172

Wakan Learning Center, c/o Rich & Charlene Svihlik, 1151 S. Humphrey Avenue, Oak Park, 60304

III. Readers

Chicago is home to hundreds of readers of all kinds—clairvoyance, tarot, astrology, past-lives, palmistry, and others. Included below is a list of those who have been publicly operating during 1975. As will become obvious, many psychics operate under professional names and have offered only their phone as a contact point.

The metropolitan area has become known for its numerous

psych-ins, at which numbers of the readers will gather for a day of readings and lectures. These events, held almost weekly, are the best place to contact a reader and also to learn who are the best. In no case should an individual present himself or herself at a reader's door without an appointment. Contact the reader for a time either by mail or phone.

Robert Abbe, P.O. Box 5608, 60680
Aengria, 837-2237; card and salt readings, life readings
Phyllis Allen, 2111 W. Sunnyside Avenue, 60625
Alphonso, Box 63, Des Plaines, 60017; chess readings
Ms. Anne, 823-3694; card readings
Miss Aradia, c/o House of Occult, 3109 N. Central Avenue, 60634; tarot
Dr. Bailos Armstrong, 6858 S. King Drive, 60637; sand readings
Art Arvesti, 722-2100
Ida Joseph Atwood, 4733 S. Forrestville Avenue, 60615; medium
Jean Austin, 510 Thorndale, Elk Grove Village, 60007; palmistry
Dorothy Barbee, 7600 N. Bosworth Avenue, 60626
Helen Beamsley, 1214 Rosedale, 60660; medium
Beatrice Beebe, 386-1741/386-4999; psychometry
Mrs. Bell, N. Clark Street at Lunt Avenue, 60626
Marlene and James Berndt, Box 522, Hoffman Estates, 60172
Betsy B., 593-7258; psychometry
Del Blair, 1315 E. 52nd Street, 60615
Elizabeth Boland, 358-3888; tarot
Mary Bowen, 10908 S. Keating, Oak Lawn, 60454; cards
Rev. Clara Boyer, 4902 N. Albany Avenue, 60625
Carter Bradley, Box 268, Prospect Heights, 60070
Herman Brostroff, 5240 N. Sheridan Road, 60640
Jean Buehrer, 434 Grant Street, Lemont, 60439
Margo Buttgereut, 5517 W. Dakin, 60641
Sister Camellia, 1138 W. Granville Avenue, 60626
Camille, 8960 Maryland Avenue, Niles, 60648
Rev. Richard Carlock, 1515 S. 51st Court, Cicero, 60650
Maria Carlyae, 530 W. Diversey Avenue (Apt. 3), 60614
Mary Chain, 586-3271
Frank Chiapatta, 9721 Avenue M, 60617
Matin Ciani, 625 N. Michigan Avenue (Suite 500), 60611
Clarion, Box 2109, 60690
Frank Clay, Jr., 224-4922
Glenn Cole, 840 Hayes Street, Gary, Ind., 46404

Nel Dalman, 310 West Hackberry Drive, Arlington Heights, 60004
Daphne, 371-3655
Mae Darling, 254-6652/995-7889
Desea Davis, 2203 N. Clybourn Avenue, 60614
Del, 1602 Ironwood Drive, Mount Prospect, 60056; palmistry
Deon, c/o Deon's Extra Sensory Perception Center, Box 3845, Merchandise Mart, 60654
Rev. Carol C. DeVise, 929-7468; tarot
Diana, c/o PSI, P.O. Box 253, Prospect Heights, 60070; tarot
Carole Doss, 4431 N. California Avenue, 60625; palmistry
Joe East, Box 5863, 60680
Evangelist Elaine, 1533 N. Wells Avenue, 60610
Joanne Ernast, 8514 W. Catalpa Avenue, 60656
Dr. Jahwer Esneit, 10431 S. Parnell Avenue 60628
Eve, Mundelein, 566-0859
Connie Fields, 230 N. Michigan Avenue (Suite 2114), 60601
Mamie Fors, 7656 S. Paulina Street, 60620
Ellida Freyer, 5410 S. Dorchester Avenue, 60615; psychic portraits
Jackie Frink, 398-9809; tarot
Kathleen Fry, 2936 W. Palmer Street, 60647; palmistry, past lives
Rev. Audrey Galeckas, 4632 S. Francisco Avenue, 60632; medium
Mary Gamble, 369 Nuttail, Riverside, 60546; palmistry
Gene, 327-7047
Miss Gerry, BA 1-1441; palmistry
Rev. George W. Gibbs, First Church of Sacred Metaphysics, 5047 S. Calumet Avenue, 60615
Gina, P.O. Box 964, Palatine, 60067; palmistry
Klara Althaus Goodrich, 5858 N. Sheridan Road, 6026; palmist
Dr. Robert Goodrich, 5858 N. Sheridan Road, 60626
Mrs. M. Green, P.O. Box 483, Barrington, 60010
Mrs. Anna Gross, 10930 Avenue M, 60617
Mary Habercamp, 1027 Windsor Road, Highland Park, 60035; domino reading
Florence Hamilton, 1213 J. Apple Lane, Elgin, 60120
Harriet of London, 17 N. State Street (Room 1514A), 60602
Helen, 7356 N. Clark Street, 60626
Louise Helene, IN 8-5337
Tom Hoefener, 407 W. Lake Street, Elmhurst, 60126

Harry Holmberg, 1706 W. Galena Boulevard, Aurora, 60506; rose readings
Alberta Houston, 666 Central Avenue, Highland Park, 60035
Irene Hughes, 500 N. Michigan Avenue, 60611
Elinora Jaksto, 2517 W. 71st Street, 60629; tarot
Jean, c/o, PSI, P.O. Box 253, Prospect Heights, 60070; biorhythm
Kirby Jefferies, 1715 E. 5th Avenue, Gary, Ind. 46401
Olga Johnson, New Age Psychic Center, 32 N. State Street (10th floor), 60602
Paul Johnson, 1701 Lake (Suite 450), Glenview, 60025
Olof Jonsson, 420 W. Wrightwood Avenue, 60614
Ralph Jordan, 761-1730
Tom Jorgensen, Aurora, 553-7274
Josephine, 535 N. Michigan Avenue, 60611
Juliana, 3109 N. Central Avenue, 60634
C. C. Just, 637-4844; tarot, palmistry
Kay, 9700 W. Armitage, Melrose Park, 60164
Henry Kent, 5517 W. Bernice Avenue, 60611
Lourice Keys, 317 Mannheim Road, Bellwood, 60104
Ann Kim, 458-7146; name readings
Kimchem, 529-3258; palmistry
Devon Kirk, 333-5488
Carole Kittering, 682-0262; numerology
Mila Kluvanek, 5915 W. Bryn Mawr Avenue, 60646
Muriel Komiss, c/o Aquarian Age Psychic Center, 3253 N. Pulaski Road, 60641; cards
Mona Konicak, 140 W. Grove, Lombard, 60148; cards
Milton Kramer, 9029 N. Columbus Drive (Bldg. 115–2D), Des Plaines, 60016
Irene Krawitz, 438 Ferndale, Glenview, 60025
Bess Krigel, 1757 W. 89th Street, 60620
Revs. Alma and Edward Krumland, 3556 W. Carmen Avenue, 60625
Randall Kryn, 1030 S. Wenonah Avenue, Oak Park, 60304
Elayne J. Kudel, 5325 Woodland, Western Springs, 60558
Len Larsen, 23 N. Reuter Drive, Arlington Heights, 60005; I Ching
Lueth Lauer, 345-6875; rune stones
Grace Lee, c/o Abacus Restaurant, 2619 N. Clark Street, 60614; face readings
Jane Levie, 246-7451; tarot
Ruth Lipp, 6944 N. Medford Avenue, 60646; cards, tea leaves

Brother Alvin Lock, 5530 S. La Salle Avenue, 60621
Gerald Loe, 206 Oak Street, Maywood, 60153; tarot
Mary Lorece, 17 N. State Street (Room 1721), 60602
Dennis McGregor, 451 South Boulevard, Oak Park 60302
Maria, GR 7-9740
Madam Maria, 62415 Damen Avenue, 60636
Ann Marro, 2114 N. Kildare Avenue, 60639
Lilyan (Leokadva) Martin, 1829 W. Larchmont Avenue, 60613
Jr. Matzer, 3400 N. Lake Shore Drive, 60657
William Mayes, 384-8598
Mel and Joyce, 259-6608
Beverly Mercer, 505 Preston Drive, Bolingbrook 60439; cards, psychometry
Michael, PSI, P.O. Box 253, Prospect Heights, 60070
Thelma Miller, 5412 N. Clark Street (Room 2, second floor), 60640
Doug Mistakus, c/o B. Krigel, 1757 W. 89th Street, 60620
Stanley J. A. Modrzyk III, 756-1113
Orchid Neal, 833 S. Humphrey Avenue, Oak Park, 60304
Bob Oertal, P.O. Box 340, Argo, 60501; palmistry
Una O'Hara, 4025 Oxford Court, Streamwood, 60103; numerology, palmistry.
R. D. Owen, 104 Deerpath, L.I.T.H., Algonquin, 60102
Terry Vance Pakula, c/o Am. Enterprises, Int., Inc., 1030 N. State Street, 60610; biorhythms
R. Dean Passmore, 6602 S. Seeley Avenue, 60636
Patricia, 253-7013
R. McKay Patterson, 4 N. Cicero Avenue (Room 204), 60644
Petri, c/o Kay's Readers' Club, 32 N. State Street, 60602
Rev. Hermine Pietkiewicz, 4400 N. Mulligan Avenue, 60630
Joseph Pinkston, 2453 N. Orchard Street, 60614
Ann Pontello, 1535 N. 33rd Avenue, Melrose Park, 60160; cards
Mary Pope, 3633 N. Ravenswood Avenue, 60613
Casmer Potynski, 7N 606 Hawthorne Lane, Medinah, 60157
Bernard B. Powell, 4118 W. 24th Place, 60623; medium
Robert Quinlivan, 3400 W. Lawrence Avenue, 60625; sand readings
Clayton E. Quinn, 656-6638
Joe O. Ramirez, Rolling Meadows, 397-1172
Molly Ranae, 1802 Locust Lane, Mount Prospect, 60056
Lilyan J. Redmond, 8135 S. Kingston Avenue, 60617

Helen L. Kientop Reed, North River Road, Box 386, Yorkville, 60560

Yolanda Reid, 787-2372

Sally Resterhouse, Skokie, 673-5068; cards

Ruth Revzen, 929-3080; palmistry

Clarence Richardson, 2907 N. Kedzie Avenue, 60618

Diane Richardson, 10526 Stowe Court, Palos Hills, 60465; tarot

Rev. Arden C. Rizer, Jr., 1666 W. Pratt Avenue, 60626; numerology

Rev. Garnet M. Rohde, 3616 N. Seeley Avenue, 60618; sand readings

Lois Rose, P.O. Box 340, Argo, 60501; palmistry

Roy Rose, P.O. Box 340, Argo, 60501

Rev. Eleanor Royse, 1961 W. Farragut Avenue, 60640; medium

Eursula Royse, c/o Foundation for Truth, 451 South Boulevard, Oak Park, 60302

Henry E. Rucker, 203 N. Wabash Avenue (Room 1820), 60601

Rev. August Schoen, 17 N. State Street (Suite 1229), 60602

Harold Schroeppel, 719 S. Clarence Avenue, Oak Park, 60304

Kathy Schofield, c/o Astro-Occult Bookshoppe, 2517 W. 71st Street, 60629

Donna Cole Schultz, 1125 W. Wellington Avenue, 60657; tarot

Alyce Bruhn Scott, 1609 S. Prospect, Park Ridge, 60068; cards

Raymond Shutay, 1031 W. Avon, Oak Lawn, 60454; cards

Pam Simonaitis, 275-5164; tarot

Dr. Gray Sims, 513 N. 10th Street, De Kalb, 60115

Elaine Sønkin (group readings only), 966-2673

Hugh Sowell, c/o First Church of Sacred Metaphysics, 5047 S. Calumet Avenue, 60615; tarot

Morika V. Stackler, 337-2404

Rev. Leni Stevens, 234-2169

Annastacia Stewart, 935 W. Winona Street, 60640; life readings

Len Swoboda, 8652 Golf Road, Des Plaines, 60016

David Techter, P.O. Box 362, Highland Park, 60035; cards

Toni, c/o Occult Book Store, 651 N. State Street, 60610

Joyce Tronson, c/o Aquarian Age Psychic Center, 3253 N. Pulaski Road, 60641

Val/Al, the Psychic Duo, 379-6824/261-8847

Lowell Van Duzee, 106 Orchard, Hillside, 60162

Ethel Wattling, 539-8345

Gary Wayne, c/o Para-Dimensions, 625 N. Michigan Avenue, 60611
Josephine and Otto Wehlen, 583-7779
Mary Williams, 5900 S. Racine Avenue, 60636; tarot
William A. Young, 4539 S. Oakenwald Avenue, 60653
William M. Young, 438-8143; aura readings
Michael R. Zaeske, Box 105, Deerfield, 60015; biorhythm
Ruth Zimmerman, Box 247, Monee, 60449
Charlotte Zuffante, 5248 W. Crystal Street, 60651

IV. Astrology

Astrology is the focus of one of the largest and most homogeneous of several groups in the Chicago psychic community. Chicago is home to a large group associated with the American Federation of Astrologers (AFA) and such nationally famous astrologers as Catherine De Jersey and Norman Arens.

GROUPS AND ORGANIZATIONS
Arcturus 23—Astrology Club, c/o Louise Bradbury, Pres., P.O. Box 283, Park Ridge, 60068
Astrological Dating Bureau, P.O. Box 512, Wheaton, 60187
Astrology Teacher's Academy, 5064 N. Lincoln Avenue, 60625
Friends of Astrology (AFA affiliate), c/o Miss Mae Kara, Ex. Sec., 4055 S. Archer Avenue, 60632
House of Sagittarius, 4218 N. Central Avenue, 60634
Old Astrologer's Shop, 2725 N. Clark Street, 60614

ASTROLOGERS
Christina Adrienne, 106 East Oak Street, 60611
Mrs. Ann, 5417 S. Pulaski Road, 60632
Norman Arens, 300 N. State Street, 60610
Astarte, 30 W. Washington Boulevard, Oak Park, 60302
Astro-Plan Inc., c/o Laurie Brady, 505 N. Lake Shore Drive, 60611
Astro Research Association, 625 N. Michigan, 60611
Astro-Trend Research Center, 556 E. 88th Place, 60619
Astro-Twin Central Registry, 2517 W. 71st Street, 60629
Sister Bessie, c/o Rosy's Candle Store, 1873 East 71st Street, 60649
Everett Blackman, 743-6792
Bert Bratt, 528-3312

Dr. *Ambrose Brierty*, 5098 S. Archer Avenue, 60632
Dorothy Cesarone, JU 9-3225
Edna B. Clark, 1704 N. Newland Avenue, 60635
Rosemary Clark, 534 Spruce Road, Bolingbrook, 60439
Henry Cole, 4250 N. Mozart Street, 60618
Katherine De Jersey, 175 E. Delaware Place, 60611
Cettie De Marco, 767-6861
Irene Diamond, 625 S. Roselle, Schaumburg, 60172
Christine Elverson, 676-1346
Eve's Horoscope Astrology Studio, 7530 Harlem, Bridgeview, 60455
John Flint, Deerfield, 945-6225
Sue Gagliardi, 627-1708
Richard J. Gordon, 5098 S. Archer Avenue, 60632
Gladys Hall, 654-0717
Mary Hall, 593-5524
Calvin Hanes, 1136 W. George Street, 60657
Doris A. Hebel, 626 N. Michigan Avenue, 60611
Melvin Higgins (Swami Kriyananda), 505 N. Michigan Avenue, 60611
Lily Ireland, 505 N. Lake Shore Drive (Apt. 5301), 60611
Roger A. Jacobson, 2245 N. Clifton, 60614
Elinora Jaksto, 2517 W. 71st Street, 60629
Mrs. Jan, 6131 S. Archer Avenue, 60638
Joyce Jensen, 837-5490
Gina Knight, P.O. Box 1252, Melrose Park, 60161
Homer R. Lathrop III, 625 N. Michigan, 60611
Sydney Lauren, 929-4178
Barbara Long, 884-1690
Brenda Lucas, 5098 S. Archer Avenue, 60632
James McDowell, Jr., 7614 S. Euclid Avenue, 60649
Harold W. McGhee, 429 North Avenue, Naperville, 60540
Judy Marco, 4739 W. Addison Street, 60641
Reverend Mary, 17 N. State Street, 60602
Mary Ann, North Avenue at Bloomingdale Road, Glen Ellyn, 60137
Toni Meier, 1206 W. Wrightwood Avenue, 60614
Cindy Miller, 1270 Taylor Avenue, Highland Park, 60035
Jackie Mulconrey, 636-6318
Thomas Neuberger, 6103 N. Seeley Avenue, 60659

Sister Page, 6241 S. Damen Avenue, 60636
Paula, 11117 S. Emerald Avenue, 60628
Arlene Petersen, 869-6426
Christine L'Origan-Rechter, 3925 N. Marshfield Avenue, 60613
Shirley Reinhardt, 334-0980
Rita's Reading and Advising, 2544 E. 79th Street, 60649
Bruce Robbins, 228 N. La Salle Street (Suite 701), 60601
Leigh Robins, 6141 N. Washtenaw Street, 60645
Teresa Roman, 281-5486
Charles Royston, Box 533, 60645
Carolyn Rupert, 18359 Hood, Homewood, 60430
Rev. E. Samuel, 17 N. State Street 60602
Richard F. Schulz, 810 Liberty Bell Court, Libertyville, 60048
Mary Seward, 637 E. Groveland Park, 60616
Bob Smith, 8809 Golf Road (Apt. 9F), Des Plaines, 60016
Vicky Snyder, 635 Parkwood, Park Ridge, 60068
Mme. V. Solovitgiz, 5917 N. Kenmore Avenue, 60660
Ron Von Steuben, 787-8220/WE 5-6589
Dee Taylor, 451 W. Melrose, 60657
Fred C. Thurman, 4740 N. Damen Avenue, 60625
Adeline Vierling, 239-5702
Richard David Wolf, 1250 W. Wrightwood Avenue, 60614
Nettie Wluzik, 13426 Avenue O, 60623
Grant Wylie, c/o Triad, 7428 N. Paulina Street, 60626

V. Graphology

The study of handwriting has become a popular part of the psychic
world and is making real progress in the business world.

ORGANIZATIONS
Abacus Handwriting Analysis Service, c/o Marle P. George, 5017
   N. Springfield Avenue, 60625
American Association of Handwriting Analysts, 1115 W. Cossitt,
   La Grange
Hallmark Handwriting Analysis, 3959 N. Lincoln Avenue, 60613
International Graphoanalysis Society, Inc., 325 W. Jackson Street,
   60606
National Guild of Professional and Business Graphologists, 18139
   S. Torrence, Lansing, 60438

APPENDIX

Alexandria, 4533 N. Whipple Street, 60625
Marie Arendt, 857-7823
Rona Barratt, 159 W. Kennedy, Streamwood, 60103
Mary Habercamp, 1027 Windsor Road, Highland Park, 60035
Paul Johnson, 1701 Lake (Suite 450), Glenview, 60025
Sharon Johnson, Route 2, Joliet, 60432
Patricia Lavin, 535 N. Michigan Avenue, 60611
Ann Pearlman, 3305 Capitol, Skokie, 60076
Jane Rizer, 1666 W. Pratt Avenue, 60626
Robert M. Schultz, 1125 W. Wellington Avenue, 60657
Gene Steccone, 619 W. Fullerton Avenue, 60614
Willy's Handwriting Analysis, 2410 122d Blue Island Avenue, 60608

VI. Hypnotism

ORGANIZATIONS
Academy of Hypnosis and Parapsychology, 5619 W. Lawrence Avenue, 60630
Association for the Promotion of Ethical Hypnotism, 100 N. La Salle Street, 60602
Center for Human Resources, 4500 Oakton, Skokie, 60076
Hypnosis Club of Chicago, 1623 W. Melrose Street, 60657
Hypnosis Counseling and Training Center, c/o Grady L. Dobbs, Box 193, Mount Prospect, 60016
Hypnosis Institute of America, 3147 Grove, Berwyn, 60402
Hypnosis Institute of Chicago, 116 S. Michigan Avenue, 60603
Institute for Rational Guidance, Ltd., 1511 S. 5th Avenue, Maywood, 60153
International Guild of Hypnotists, Inc., 410 S. Michigan Avenue, 60605
National Hypnotic Research Center, P.O. Box 933, Arlington Heights, 60006
Universal Hypnotic Institute, Inc., 6100 W. Gunnison Street, 60630

HYPNOTISTS
Norman Boss, 714 E. Algonquin Road, Arlington Heights, 60005
David Burke, 1606 Columbia Bay Road, Villa Park, 60046
Barbara Christensen, KE 9-4051
Ed Dalman, 310 W. Heckberry Drive, Arlington Heights, 60004

Lee M. Darrow, 848-5008
Del, 1602 Ironwood Drive, Mount Prospect, 60056
Grady Dobbs, 640 Murray Lane, Des Plaines, 60016
Adrian Finkelstein, 855 E. Palatine Road, Palatine, 60067
Lee J. Fitzpatrick 867 N. Dearborn Parkway, 60610
Larry Garrett, 5619 W. Lawrence Street, 60630
Elinora Jaksto, 2517 W. 71st Street, 60629
Marlene Koumbis, Skokie, 679-3138
Dom J. Locascio, 4912 W. Iowa Street, 60651
Patrick C. McAuley, 8 S. Michigan Avenue, 60603; medical hypnosis
Max Melzer, 1762 W. Thome Avenue, 60626
E. A. Mendyk, 3919 W. 47th Street, 60632
Dr. Milton A. Saffir, 55 E. Washington Street, 60602
Dr. Jordan M. Scher, 8 S. Michigan Avenue, 60603; medical hypnosis
Marie Vole, 5619 W. Lawrence Avenue, 60630
Joan Walker, 4518 W. Shore Drive, McHenry, 60050

VII. Non-Conventional Healing

Possibly the most pervasive activity in the psychic community is "healing" in its various forms. There is present among psychically oriented people a tremendous interest in alternatives to allopathic medicine, and many psychics do healing as a matter of course. There is usually a hesitancy to charge for healing efforts; hence, there are few full-time practitioners, except for those involved in various non-allopathic medicines, such as chiropractic, osteopathy, etc. Among those who have become known as "healers" there is a wide variety of explanations as to how healing works. Most would, however, see the active agent as a power (Holy Spirit, Universal Force, Prana) which passes through the "healer" into the "patient."

Particular note should be taken by the reader that inclusion in the list below is *not* to be taken as an endorsement of those listed or of any claims which they might make. Persons wishing the services of a "healer" should investigate each for himself or herself.

National Shrine of St. Ann, 2715 W. 38th Place, 60632
Shrine of the Healing Trinity, c/o Gene Maurey, 4555 W. 60th Street, 60629
Spiritual Healers League, 5033 W. 25th Place, 60650

Glenn Cole, 840 Hayes Street, Gary, Indiana, 46404
Mary Doherty, 4544 S. Saint Louis Avenue, 60632
Don Easterberg, 2152 Pioneer Road, Evanston, 60201
Robert D. Ericsson, c/o Spiritual Advisory Council, 1701 Lake
   (Suite 450), Glenview, 60025
Rev. Audrey Galeckas, 4632 S. Francisco Avenue, 60632
Ruth Lipp, 6944 N. Medford Avenue, 60646
Gerald M. Loe, 206 Oak Street, Maywood, 60153
Madonna Herrod, 774-0430
Ethel Lombardi, c/o Spiritual Advisory Council, 1071 Lake (Suite
   450), Glenview, 60025
Gordon and Dorothea Melton, Box 1311, Evanston, 60201
Rosita Rodriguez, 714 S. Scoville Avenue, Oak Park, 60304
Rev. Eleanor Royse, 1961 W. Farragut Avenue, 60640
Henry Rucker, Room 1820, 203 N. Wabash Avenue, 60601
John Scudder, 1353 Olive, Homewood, 60430
Rev. Charlotte Zuffante, 5248 W. Crystal Street, 60651

NON-ALLOPATHIC MEDICINE
Many people are not aware of the numerous options for medical
treatment available to them. In the Chicago metropolitan area, however, there are a wide variety of medical practices. Physicians engaged in chiropractic, naprapathy, naturopathy, and osteopathy can
be found in the yellow pages of the phone book. For references,
the reader may wish to contact the schools and pharmacies for
each group.
Acu-Moon Academy of Acupuncture, P.O. Box 1124, Evanston,
   60201
Chicago General Health Services (chiropractic), 1615 W. Warren
   Avenue, 60607
National College of Chiropractic, 200 E. Roosevelt, Lombard,
   60148
Ehrhart & Karl Pharmacies (homeopathic), 17 N. Wabash Avenue,
   60602
Chicago National College of Naprapathy, 3330 N. Milwaukee Avenue, 60641
Chicago College of Osteopathic Medicine, 1122 E. 53rd Street,
   60615
Reflexology (Ingham Method), Kathy M. Heaton, 1N 253 Bloom-
   ingdale Road, Wheaton, 60187

The New Thought tradition of mental healing, or Christian Science, has produced a major form of spiritual healing. The largest of the mental healing bodies, the Church of Christ, Scientist, has many workers in the Chicago area and can be found listed in the yellow pages under "Christian Science Practitioners."

Christian Science, c/o First Church of Christ, Scientist, and Reading Room, 1111 S. Wabash Avenue, 60605

Visiting Nurse Service for Christian Scientists in the Greater Chicago Area, 104 N. Oak Park Avenue, Oak Park, 60301

There are eight congregations of the Unity School of Christianity in the Chicago area. For information and local addresses contact:

Christ Way Unity Church and Book Room, 410 S. Michigan Avenue, 60605.

Other centers include:

Evanston Divine Science Center, c/o Dr. Bernadette Turner, Hotel Sovereign, 60626;

First Church of Religious Science, c/o Dr. Carleton Whitehead, 936 N. Michigan Avenue, 60611 (services held at 54 E. Oak Street);

First Divine Science Church, 8 S. Michigan Avenue (Suite 312), 60603;

Temple of Divine Science, 1326 E. 63rd Street, 60637.

VIII. Spiritual, Mystical, Meditative, and Religious Groups

Within the larger psychic community, the growth of Eastern religions has been a major force since the late-nineteenth century, when the influence of the Theosophical Society began to be felt. In the late 1960s and early 1970s these Eastern-oriented groups expanded and were joined by the pagan and magical bodies. Chicago stands in a unique position in regard to these bodies, most of which are Eastern imports. While being home to several unique groups itself, Chicago is the first stopping spot of groups from both coasts as they cross the country.

Several of the groups listed below have made specific denial of their religious nature. In each case such denial involves a semantic problem over what is meant by "religious." The Student International Meditation Society (which goes under various designations of the Transcendental Meditation umbrella) has denied any designation as "religious," "psychic," or "spiritual." With all due respect to their protests, the fact that many members of various religious groups have profited from TM, and their own literature, which presents a distinct metaphysical world view, tend to refute their public position.

Included below are the full range of groups, including Santanic (of a non-LaVey variety), the national headquarters of the I AM, Eastern groups of both Buddhist and Hindu origins, and psychic groups with a wide variety of perspectives.

Akbar Theosophical Center, 63 E. Adams Street (4th Floor), 60603

American Federation of Young Theosophists, Box 270, Wheaton, 60187

Ananda Marga, 6439 N. Leavitt Avenue, 60645

Arica Institute, Inc., 110 S. Dearborn Avenue (Suite 220), 60603

Babaji Yoga Sangam, 1118 W. Armitage Street, 60614

Calumet Pagan Temple, 1519 Kennilworth, Calumet City, 60409

Chicago Dharmadhatu, 640 N. State Street, 60610

Chicago Zendo (Renzai), 472-4810

Christian Community (Steiner), 1409 N. Dearborn Street, 60610

Christian Spiritual Alliance, 2112 N. Kildare Avenue, 60639

Church of St. Francis (Liberal Catholic), 1945 N. Mozart Street, 60647

Church of Scientology of Illinois, 1555 Maple Avenue, Evanston, 60201

Congregation of Aten (Egyptian), 2809 S. Trumbull Avenue, 60623

Cosmic Circle of Fellowship, P.O. Box A3179, 60690

Dianetic Research Foundation, 121 E. Oak Street, 60611

Divine Light Mission, 7558 N. Rogers Park Boulevard, 60626

Eckankar, Chicago Satsang Society, 5366 N. Milwaukee Avenue, 60630

Essence of Hermetic Light Church, The Penthouse, 27 East Monroe Street, 60603

First Temple of the Craft of W.I.C.A., 2735 Chicago Road, South Chicago Heights, 60411

Foundation Church of the Millennium, 1529 N. Wells Street, 60610

Foundation Studies (Steiner), c/o Thomas Brayman, 529 Grant Place, 60614

3HO (Healthy, Happy, Holy Organization; Kundalini Yoga), 826 W. Newport Avenue, 60657; or 7531 S. Dorchester Avenue, 60619

Hare Krishna Temple (ISKCON), 1014 Emerson Street, Evanston, 60201

Himalayan International Institute of Yoga Science and Philosophy (Swami Rama), 1505 Greenwood Road, Glenview, 60025

Holy Order of Mans, 2328 N. Oakley Avenue, 60647; Thrift Shop, 2110 N. Damen Avenue, 60647; Innerlight Community, 5775 N. Ridge Avenue, 60626

I AM Temple and Reading Room, 176 W. Washington Street, 60602

J. Krishnamurti Group, c/o Jagdish, 973-4278

Meher Baba Information Center, 410 S. Michigan Avenue (Room 1025), 60605

Narayanananda Universal Yoga Trust and Ashrama in America, 9435 S. 85th Court (Apt. E-1), Hickory Hills, 60457

Neo-Pythagorean Gnostic Church, c/o Michael Berteaux, P.O. Box 1554, 60690

Ontological Society, c/o Mr. and Mrs. Sheldon F. Blechman, RR ⅝2, Box 109, Mundelein, 60060

Order of Rhea, 1125 W. Wellington Avenue, 60657

Principles of Inner Life and Peace Association, Inc., c/o Louis E. Arias, 100 W. Chicago Avenue, 60610

Pristine Egyptian Orthodox Church, 5017–15 N. Clark Street, 60640

The Process, c/o Richard Price, 1945 N. Burling Street, 60614

Radha Soami Beas, c/o Mrs. Marjorie Reed, 803 N. Oak Park Avenue, Oak Park, 60302

Real Yoga Society, c/o Swami Shiva, 47 Harrison Street, Oak Park, 60304

Rosicrucian Order (AMORC) Reading Room, 2539 N. Kedzie Avenue, 60647

Sabaean Order of Amn, c/o Frederic De Arechaga, 2447 N. Halsted Street, 60614

Shree Gurudev Sadhana Center, c/o Ann Kahala, 4621 Stonewall, Downers Grove, 60515

Silent Prayer Sanctuary, c/o Rev. Sophia Schaffer, 6343 W. Cuyler Avenue, 60634

Sri Chinmoy Center, c/o Mr. Sandy Balter, 1629 S. Michigan Avenue, Villa Park, 60181

Stelle Group, Box 5900, 60680

Student International Meditation Society: Evanston World Plan Center, 604 Davis Street, Evanston, 60201; Chicago City World Plan Center, 11 W. Delaware Place, 60610

Summit Lighthouse, P.O. Box 266, Lemont, 60439

Temple of Kriya Yoga, 505 N. Michigan Avenue, 60611

Temple of Power, Box 134, Deerfield, 60015

Thee Satanic Church, 1733 N. 18th Avenue, Melrose Park, 60160

Thee Satanic Orthodox Church of Nethilum Rites, 3109 N. Central Avenue, 60634

Theosophical Society of America, 1926 N. Main, Box 270, Wheaton, 60187

Universal Meditation Center, 957 E. 75th Street, 60619

Urantia Foundation, 533 W. Diversey Parkway, 60614

Uranus Temple, 1125 W. Wellington Avenue, 60657

Vivekananda Vedanta Society of Chicago, 5423 S. Hyde Park Boulevard, 60615

Zazen Group, Buddhist Educational Center of the Buddhist Temple of Chicago, 4645 N. Racine Avenue, 60640

Zen Temple of Chicago, 2330 N. Halsted Street, 60614

YOGA GROUPS

Besides the groups listed above there are several that specialize in yoga, usually *hatha,* but many also offer *raja* (meditation).

International Institute of Shinsundo, 3315 N. Clark Street, 60657

Janyce Hamilton Yoga Today, 1043 Waukegan Road, Glenview, 60025

Judy Yoga Says, Box 144, Lombard, 60148

Mind and Body Systems, 5344 W. Devon Avenue, 60646

Sohom Yoga Center, 63 E. Adams Street, 60603

Yoga Inc., 20 Yorkshire Woods, Oak Brook, 60521

Yoga International, 729 Sheridan, Winthrop Harbor, 60096

Yoga Meditation Society of Evanston, c/o Sadhana Brahmacarini (Lydia A. Smith), 1515 Sherman Avenue, Evanston, 60201

Yoga Retreat, 57 E. Walton Street, 60611

Yogi Sri Nerode of India, 5442 S. Dorchester Avenue, 60615

APPENDIX

IX. Spiritualist Churches

This survey has been able to locate over eighty spiritualist churches; and in all likelihood, there are others in the suburbs. The spiritualists, though strong, have lost the thrust of the psychic community to the "psych-ins," which are held on Sunday, and to forms of psychic life that emphasize development, healing, and spiritual philosophy rather than spirit communication. Spiritualism is strongest in the black community, where most churches bear the name "Spiritual" and operate from storefronts. The National Spiritualist Association of Churches remains strong in the white community.

Illinois State Spiritualist Association (NSAC), c/o Rev. Ernest Schoenfeld, Pres., 3501 Shakespeare Avenue, 60647

Abraham Household of Faith, 1239 S. Kedzie Avenue, 60623

All Nations House of Prayer, c/o Rev. Flora Collins, 5148 W. Madison Street, 60644

Beulah Land Temple of Faith, 1015 W. 61st Street, 60621

Cathedral Temple of Divine Love, c/o Rev. Peter J. Brown, Jr., 6708 S. Stoney Island Avenue, 60649

Christ Church of Universal Law, c/o Rev. Arthur V. Martin, 928 Rollins Road, Round Lake Heights, 60073

Christabelle Spiritualist Church, (NSAC), c/o Ben D. Jones, Jr., 200 Willow Avenue, Joliet, 60436

Church of Divine Revelation, Midland Hotel, 172 W. Adams Street, 60603

Church of Harmony, Rev. Ethel Weltz, 1110 N. Sheridan Road, Peoria, 61606

Church of the Spirit, c/o Rev. Ernest Schoenfeld, 2651 N. Central Park Avenue, 60647

Cicero First Spiritual Church, 5033 W. 25th Place, Cicero, 60650

Cosmopolitan Church of Prayer, Rev. Luther Charles G. Hayes, 6315 S. Langley Avenue, 60637

David Spiritual Temple, c/o Bishop Burton, 4225 S. Vincennes Avenue, 60653

Divine Spiritual Temple, 3850 S. Ellis Avenue, 60653

Egypt Temple of God, 555 E. 71st Street, 60619

Emmanuel Healing Temple, c/o Rev. Nina McGuire, 613 E. 43rd Street, 60653

Everlasting Gospel Spiritual Church, c/o Rev. B. Taylor, 527 E. 71st Street, 60619

Everlasting Life Spiritual Church, c/o Bishop B. Collins, 750 W. 69th Street, 60621

Faith Temple Community Church, 2245 W. Roosevelt Road, 60608

First Church of Deliverance, c/o Rev. Clarence H. Cobbs, 4315 S. Wabash Avenue, 60653

First Church of Sacred Metaphysics, c/o Rev. George W. Gibbs, 5047 S. Calumet Avenue, 60615

First Spiritualist Church, c/o Ellen Stopa, 5033 W. 25th Place, Cicero, 60650

First Spiritualist Church of Joliet, c/o Rev. Myrtle M. Sperry, Glenwood Place & Jasper Street, Joliet, 60436

First Temple of Universal Law, c/o Rev. Charlotte Bright, 5030 N. Drake Avenue, 60625

Flower Candlelight Guide Spiritual Church, 4042 N. Western Avenue, 60618

Friendly Church of Christ, 2436 N. Western Avenue, 60647

Golden Rule Church, c/o Rev. Anna Zalckar, 549 N. Cicero Avenue, 60644

Good Shepherd Spiritual Church, 7131 S. Halsted Street, 60621

Grace Temple Community Church, 5717 W. Madison Street, 60644

Greater Mt. Calvary Spiritual Church, 3434 W. Roosevelt Road, 60624

Healing Temple of Christ, c/o Reverend Beulah, 19 E. 69th Street, 60637

Holy Family Spiritual Temple, c/o Bishop J. L. Gardner, 4107 W. Roosevelt Road, 60624

Holy Spiritual Temple No. 11, c/o Rev. Otis Cunningham, 4661 S. State Street, 60609

House of Prayer, 2200 S. Pulaski Road, 60623

Ideal Love and Faith Temple, 1107 W. 63rd Street, 60621

Immanuel Church, c/o Rev. Louis B. King, 73 Park Drive, Glenview, 60025

Jacob's Healing Temple, 5859 S. Wabash Avenue, 60637

Lily of the Valley Spiritual Church, c/o Rev. Lucretia Smith, 257 W. 48th Place, 60609

Little Friendly Spiritual Church, c/o Rev. O. Payne, 7020 S. Racine Avenue, 60636

The Lord's House of Prayer, 5910 S. State Street, 60621

Louis Uher Memorial Church, c/o Rev. Emily V. & Rev. Fred C. Ludmann, 2614 N. Austin Avenue, 60639

Love and Faith House of Prayer, 4645 W. Madison Street, 60644

Love and Faith Mission, c/o Rev. Hattie Swanson, 626 S. Western Avenue, 60612

Mercy Healing Temple, 3141 W. Roosevelt Road, 60612

Mission of the Divine Word, c/o Rev. Charles White, 6406 S. Carpenter Street, 60621

Mt. Sinai Divine Temple of Truth, 7412 S. Vincennes Avenue, 60621

New Hope Spiritual Church, c/o Rev. Isadore Scruggs, 7240 S. Racine Avenue, 60636

Northbrook Mission of Universal Law, Rev. Wanda McLenahan, 17 Pine Tree Road, Northbrook, 60062

Our Lady Mother of the Church Parish, 8701 W. Leland Avenue, 60656

Puritan Spiritualist Church, 10957 S. King Drive

Puritan Spiritualist Church, c/o Anna Gross, 13906 Green Bay Avenue, Burnham, 60633

Redeeming Church of Christ, c/o Rev. James L. Anderson, 6920 S. Harper Avenue, 60637

Righteous Supreme Temple of God, 3821 S. Wabash Avenue, 60653

Rising Sun Spiritual Church, 154 E. Marquette Road, 60637

Rose Don Chapel, 3629 W. 123rd Street, 60658

Rose of Sharon Spiritual Church, Rev. Rose Bridges, 4003 W. Monroe Street, 60624

St. John Spiritual Church of the Soul, c/o Rev. Joseph E. Brown, 4342 S. Cottage Grove Avenue, 60653

St. Jude's Spiritual Temple, c/o Rev. Annie Boles, 1653 W. Washington Street, 60612

St. Jude Vineyard Spiritual Temple, 1202 W. 69th Street, 60636

St. Mary's Healing Temple, 317 S. Cicero Avenue, 60644

St. Mary's Spiritual Church, 1343 S. Newberry Avenue, 60608

St. Paul Divine Healing Spiritual Church, c/o Reverend Stiles, 749 W. 61st Street, 60621

St. Paul's Spiritual Church, c/o Rev. Louise Quinn, 1549 N. Cicero Avenue, 60651

St. Thomas Spiritual Church, 554 E. 43rd Street, 60653

St. Veronica Spiritual Church, 3859 W. Roosevelt Road, 60624

Sharon Church, c/o Rev. Robert H. P. Cole, 5220 N. Wayne Avenue, 60640

Silent Prayer Sanctuary, c/o Rev. Sophia Schaffer, 3602 W. McLean Avenue, 60647

Simpson's Chapel Spiritual Church, 7504 S. Cottage Grove Avenue, 60619

Spiritual Church of Truth, c/o Kathryn Duha, 3349 W. North Avenue, 60647

Spiritual Science Church No. 3, c/o Rev. Mildred J. Pekul, 1715 W. 64th Street, 60637

Spiritualist Church of Divinity, c/o Rev. Mary E. Novak, 4118 W. 24th Place, 60623

Spiritualist Church of Truth, c/o Rev. Theodore Siers, 3349 W. North Avenue, 60647

Spiritualist Temple of Immortality, c/o Rev. Harry Erickson, 1700 W. 51st Street, 60609

Supreme Spiritual Center, c/o Rev. Charles Lee, 4310 W. Monroe Street, 60624

Swedenborgian Church, 5710 S. Woodlawn Avenue, 60637

Swedenborgian General Church and Book Room, c/o Rev. Robert H. P. Cole, 5220 N. Wayne Avenue, 60640

Tabernacle Church of Perfect Love, Incorporated and Spiritual, 1539 S. Christiana Avenue, 60623

Temple of Cosmic Rays, c/o Rev. H. Swanson, 1423 W. Augusta Boulevard, 60622

Temple of God, c/o Mother Esther Williams, 735 E. 47th Street, 60653

Temple of Life, c/o Rev. S. Page, 6241 S. Damen Avenue, 60636; and 1400 S. Michigan Avenue, 60605

Temple of Light Spiritualist Church, 451 W. South Boulevard, Oak Park, 60302

Templo Voces Espirituales, c/o Juan Alverio, 2475 N. Clybourn Avenue, 60614

Traveling Soul Spiritualist Church, c/o Rev. Mercedes H. Pitcher, 1124 S. Independence Boulevard, 60623

The True Temple of Solomon Church, c/o Rev. Eddie Banks, 7138 S. Halsted Street, 60621

True Temple of Truth, c/o Rev. Valean Adams, 1649 W. 79th Street, 60620

Tucker Smith Memorial Spiritualist Temple, c/o Louise Washington, 6146 Ashland Avenue, 60636

United Kingdom of Christ, c/o Rt. Rev. Errold P. Johnson, 6234
   S. Ashland Avenue, 60636
Upper Room Spiritual Church, 3432 W. Roosevelt Road, 60624
Wesley Chapel Church, 4812 W. Madison Street, 60644
White Cloud Holy Church, c/o Bishop Ratliff, 4249 W. Cermak
   Road, 60623

X. UFO and Related Groups

Chicago is home to the most significant UFO group presently in
existence. It is headed by Dr. J. Allen Hynek of Northwestern Uni-
versity and has picked up the study no longer being supported by
the government.
Center for UFO Studies, c/o Dr. J. Allen Hynek, P.O. Box 11,
   Northfield, 60093
Other:
Ancient Astronaut Society, 600 Talcott Road, Park Ridge, 60068
Chicago Fortean Circle (of the International Fortean Organi-
   zation), c/o Richard T. Crowe, P.O. Box 29054, 60629

XI. Resources: Books and Supplies

The size of any psychic community can usually be measured by the
number of bookstores that offer a large selection of psychic books
and occult supplies. Chicago has its share and is also home to a
number of publishers of both books and periodicals (though New
York City and Los Angeles are the major centers of the publishing
industry). Chicago has a large Latin American community and has
numerous *botánicos,* which sell the implements necessary for practitioners of *Santería* and *Voodoo.* For a list of the *botánicos* see the
yellow pages under "religious supplies."

PUBLISHERS
Clark Publishing Company (FATE magazine), 500 Hyacinth
   Place, Highland Park, 60035
Stellium Press (books and pamphlets), Box 1311, Evanston, 60201
Theosophical Publishing House, P.O. Box 270, Wheaton, 60189
Yogi Publication Society, Box 148, Des Plaines, 60016

RETAIL OUTLETS
Astro-Occult Book Shoppe, 2517 W. 71st Street, 60629
Dilley Co. (pyramids), 9232 S. Sawyer Avenue, 60642

El Sabarum, 2447 N. Halsted Street, 60614
House of Knowledge, 652 S. Roselle, Schaumburg, 60172
House of Occult, 3109 N. Central Avenue, 60634
House of Sagittarius, 4218 N. Central Avenue, 60634
International Psychic Center, 1733 N. 18th Street, Melrose Park, 60160
Lost Horizons, 8019 W. Ogden, Lyons, 60534
Motivation Development Bookstore, 1701 N. Lake (Suite 450), Glenview, 60025
The Mystic Eye, 3250 Market Plaza, The Mall, Kirchoff Road, Rolling Meadows, 60008
Occult Bookstore, 615 N. State Street, 60610
Old Astrologer's Shop, 2725 N. Clark Street, 60614
Osiris Book Service, Ltd., P.O. Box A3043-BC, 60690
Palmer's Astrology and Yoga Center, 711 Sunset Lane, Joliet, 60436
Posters Plus, 2709 W. 71st Street, 60629
Pyramid Cos-Models, 3274 W. Fullerton Avenue, 60647
Sanctus Spiritus, 2735 Chicago Road, South Chicago Heights, 60411
Spiritual Frontiers Fellowship, 800 Custer Avenue, Evanston, 60202
Temple Book Store (Kriya Yoga), 510 N. Michigan Avenue, 60611
Temple Book Store (Uranus), 1125 W. Wellington Avenue, 60657
Venture Bookshop, P.O. Box 247, Highland Park, 60035

PERIODICALS

The Alpha Star, c/o A. J. Benchly, 5959 S. Kenneth Avenue, 60629
The American Theosophist, Box 270, Wheaton, 60187
Ancient Skies, c/o Ancient Astronaut Society, 600 Talcott Road, Park Ridge, 60068
Fate, 500 Hyacinth Place, Highland Park, 60035
Midwest Psychic News, 2517 West 71st Street, 60629
Parapsychology Now, 183 Grissom Lane, Hoffman Estates, 60172
Sophia, c/o Rosemary Clark, 534 Spruce Road, Bolingbrook, 60439
Temple Messenger, First Temple of Universal Law, 5030 N. Drake Avenue, 60625

APPENDIX